ISSUES THAT CONCERN YOU

Teens and Employment

Heidi Watkins, *Book Editor*

GREENHAVEN PRESS
A part of Gale, Cengage Learning

GALE
CENGAGE Learning™

Detroit • New York • San Francisco • New Haven, Conn • Waterville, Maine • London

Christine Nasso, *Publisher*
Elizabeth Des Chenes, *Managing Editor*

© 2011 Greenhaven Press, a part of Gale, Cengage Learning

For more information, contact:
Greenhaven Press
27500 Drake Rd.
Farmington Hills, MI 48331-3535
Or you can visit our Internet site at gale.cengage.com

Articles in Greenhaven Press anthologies are often edited for length to meet page require-ments. In addition, original titles of these works are changed to clearly present the main thesis and to explicitly indicate the author's opinion. Every effort is made to ensure that Greenhaven Press accurately reflects the original intent of the authors. Every effort has been made to trace the owners of copyrighted material.

Cover image photos.com / Getty Images.

LIBRARY OF CONGRESS CATALOGING-IN-PUBLICATION DATA

Teens and employment / Heidi Watkins, book editor.
    p. cm. -- (Issues that concern you)
 Includes bibliographical references and index.
 ISBN 978-0-7377-5208-3 (hardcover)
 1. Teenagers--Employment--Juvenile literature. 2. Youth-Employment--Juvenile literature. I. Watkins, Heidi.
  HD6270.T44 2011
  331.3'47--dc22

                                                    2010048603

Printed in the United States of America
 2 3 4 5 6 7 15 14 13 12 11

CONTENTS

Delaney Allen-Mills, a high school senior and school newspaper photographer, supplemented her allowance by taking pictures at children's birthday parties. Once the recession hit, however, the photography jobs dried up. During the holiday hiring season of 2009, she looked for work at a large, nearby mall, the fifth-largest shopping center in the United States. About twenty-one shops were hiring, but most would not even give an application to anyone under eighteen.

Devine Ford dropped out of high school in eighth grade and found work at a Popeye's restaurant. A year later, however, he lost his job after being arrested for driving without a license. After that, Devine applied for more than one hundred positions, but he did not receive even one telephone call.

Juan Iraheta, nineteen, despite not finishing high school, was getting by working for Best Buy, but then his hours were cut and his manager warned of impending layoffs. Supporting his girlfriend and their two-year-old son, he began desperately looking for a full-time job or a job that would allow him to go back to school.

Teens have been hit particularly hard by unemployment for various reasons. They are consistently crowded out of jobs by older workers who have been laid off or who are unable to retire. In addition, teens often seek employment by companies in retail, manufacturing, and construction, sectors that have been significantly affected by the recession. According to a January 2010 article in *Time* magazine, teen unemployment rates are three times that of adult unemployment rates. In fact, says Andrew Sum, head of the Center for Labor Market Studies at Northeastern University and a nationally recognized expert on teen employment, "Proportionally, more kids have lost jobs in the past few years than the entire country lost in the Great Depression."[1] A March 2010 *St. Louis Dispatch* article citing a study from the same university conveys bleak statistics: Unemployment rates are 9.7 percent overall, 26.2 percent for teens as of December 2009, and nearly 50 percent for African American teens.

Teen unemployment is a serious issue, one that affects some more than others. For some teens, having a job is the only way they can afford college entrance exams and college textbooks; other teens have scholarships or parents to cover the costs. For some teens, unemployment means postponing college or taking out large college loans and going to college anyway in the hope that a degree will help secure a decent job. For some teens, being out of work means having to remain dependent on relatives who may or may not be willing or able to provide for them.

Perhaps the teens who face the biggest threat from unemployment are the thirty thousand who age out of foster care each year when they reach their eighteenth birthdays. According to the organization Honoring Emancipated Youth, in 2006—even prior to the recession—80 percent of former foster care kids did not earn enough to fully support themselves four years after leaving foster care. Similarly, a major study released April 7, 2010, by Chapin Hall at the University of Chicago and Partners for Our Children at the University of Washington revealed that a large majority of teens who age out of the foster care system still do not make a smooth transition into the world of work.

The study followed hundreds of foster care kids and non-foster care kids from age seventeen or eighteen to age twenty-three or twenty-four. At the end of the study, 72 percent of those who had not been in foster care were working. Of the former foster care kids, however, only 48 percent were working, and furthermore, their median annual income was only eight thousand dollars. A study of former foster care kids from 2007 found that over 90 percent of those surveyed had earned less than ten thousand dollars over the previous year.

The benefits of employment are not just financial. Employment can give teens the focus, self-worth, motivation, and discipline that encourage them to complete school. While approximately three-quarters of the former foster care kids in the 2010 study had completed their high school education or earned their general

Teen unemployment rates were three times higher than those of adults in 2010.

equivalency diploma, only 6 percent of them had finished a two- or four-year college degree by age twenty-four.

The good news is that even though unemployment is worse than ever, because of studies like these just cited, federal and state governments and community groups are stepping up their efforts to support teens and young adults past the age of eighteen. A new federal law allows states access to more federal funding if states allow young people to stay in the foster care system during young adulthood. Some states are also providing more college scholarships, job training programs, and transitional programs. Community groups are providing care packages with everything from bedsheets to pots and pans for those venturing out on their own for the first time.

Teens in foster care represent just one population of young people for whom employment is critically important. The selections in *Issues That Concern You: Teens and Employment* represent multiple viewpoints surrounding the issue, revealing its significance and complexity. In addition, the volume contains several appendixes to help the reader understand and explore the topic, including a thorough bibliography and a list of organizations to contact for further information. The appendix titled "What You Should Know About Teens and Employment" offers facts about teens' rights and protections in the workplace. The appendix "What You Should Do About Teens and Employment" provides tips for young people seeking work. With such features, *Issues That Concern You: Teens and Employment* constitutes a sound resource for those interested in this issue.

Notes

1. Stephen Gandel, "In a Tough Job Market, Teens Are Suffering Most," *Time*, January 18, 2010. www.time.com/time/magazine/article/0,9171,1952331,00.html.

ONE

Employment Offers Teens Valuable Experiences

Jennifer Nelson

Typically, teens look for summer or part-time jobs so they can earn spending money or save money for college. Jennifer Nelson, a writer for *Career World*, a magazine for middle and high school students, presents other important benefits of teen employment. Learning to manage money and a new appreciation for the value of a dollar is one benefit. Other benefits include gaining skills such as customer service, communication, and responsibility—skills required for success in any occupation. Nelson also encourages teens to think beyond fast-food jobs and to look for entry-level employment in fields in which they are interested. An entry-level job in any given field provides the opportunity to see firsthand what life is like in that field and the different types of careers available within it.

Mallory Gray is figuring it all out. She doesn't quite know exactly what her future career will be, but she's on the right track. The 17-year-old from Springfield, Mo., has already had two fairly unusual part-time jobs. "I really just wanted to get a feel for different things," she says. Last year [2004], she groomed, exercised, and showed horses at a thoroughbred auction. Today, she

Jennifer Nelson, "Beyond the Mall: Great Jobs for Teens Are Out There—Learn How to Make One of Them Yours!" *Career World,* a Weekly Reader Publication, October 2005, pp. 18–22. Reprinted by permission.

works part-time as a food-service technician at a hospital, where she delivers food trays to patients. She's also picturing herself building a career in health care.

Mallory thought about being a doctor when she was little and still thinks it could be an option. Her part-time job is helping her decide. "Even though I specialize in food and nutrition, I'm still around doctors and nurses," Mallory points out. She watches how medical professionals do their jobs; she interacts with patients and has learned her way around a hospital—things that may help her decide on that medical career. "I know it isn't as glamorous as *ER* on television, but I could still have fun with it and help people," she says. Pediatrics and surgery are two areas she's now considering.

Why Work Now?

More than half of high school seniors, 56 percent, said they worked in the spring of their final year of school, with most earning minimum wage, according to a study by the University of Washington. Nationwide, about two out of five teens ages 16 to 19 hold a part-time job. Retail gigs and burger joints are the jobs teens have traditionally gravitated toward, since they're close to home, convenient to school, or often the only options available. But if, like Mallory, you're exploring your future career options or simply want to work with something you have a passion for—cars, for instance—there are opportunities to bust out of the box.

"Whether you're bagging groceries, working at an amusement park, or painting houses, it's never too early to start honing marketable skills and building a strong resume," says Sharon Rosengart, director of career services at DeVry University in North Brunswick, N.J. Rosengart suggests taking on as much responsibility as possible and finding creative ways to get the most out of your part-time, after-school, or summer job. If you are enthusiastic about your work, aren't afraid to put your originality on display, and step up to the difficult tasks no one else wants, you'll earn the respect of your employers—and they can help you with networking and provide references later on.

The benefits of a part-time job include making and spending your own money, developing a sense of responsibility, and gaining skills.

How Part-Time Work Pays Off

There are serious benefits in any part-time job: First, you'll make your own money (cool for sure), but you'll also be responsible for deciding how to spend and save those greenbacks. You'll need to make decisions—for example, do you really need another lip gloss or a pair of expensive tennis shoes? Or should you save up to buy a car or to pay that cell phone bill due at the end of the month?

"Another thing that's valuable is gaining soft skills," says Rosengart. These aren't technical skills required for your job but all the other things your day-to-day work may involve—like written and verbal communication, dealing with customers, handling money, putting people at ease, managing your time, relating to someone who may not speak English well, or dealing with kids.

John Gaeta, 17, of St. Petersburg, Fla., is gaining a lot of important skills he can use in the future. He's put his love of water and swimming to good use by taking a lifeguard certification course and snagging a job at an area pool. Lifeguarding has taught John about dealing with the public, communicating well, and handling daily responsibilities. "At any second, someone's life may be in danger and I have to act quickly to ensure their safety," he says.

John has learned how to react in tough situations—rowdy kids, unhappy patrons, people who need to be put at ease quickly. He notes that his lifeguarding job "has given me good experience working with others and taught me how I need to respond calmly but differently in every situation." John is interested in a career in sales—and he knows the skills and experience he's gained as a lifeguard will be useful in almost any career.

How to Find That Job

If you're prowling for a cool part-time job, start by writing down your skills, talents, strengths, weaknesses, hobbies, likes, and dislikes, says Jeanne Webster, author of *If You Could Be Anything, What Would You Be? A Teen's Guide to Mapping Out the Future* (Dupuis North Publishing, 2004). That list can help you determine the kind of job you'd be most happy doing.

Then it's time to spring into action and find that job. Think about the businesses you and your family use most often: veterinarians, accountants, repair shops. What skills do you have that they could use? Once you have a specific job idea in mind, contact the businesses and offer your services.

Network with people you know. Let everyone—parents, friends, neighbors, your brother's friend's dad—know that you are looking for work. Make sure you tell them the kind of job you're seeking.

Kim Oates, 18, of Jacksonville, Fla., found her job when a friend mentioned that her mom's salon needed a receptionist. "Working in a salon fits me well, since I love sampling the products, seeing people's transformations, and keeping up on the latest styles and trends," says Oates. She checks clients in and out, handles a computerized appointment schedule and cash register, makes reminder calls, does shampoos, and assists the stylists with mixing color and perm solutions.

"I've learned a lot about giving customers what they want," she says. Oates has honed marketable skills in keeping clients happy, staying organized, and working with a team of people. She's even thought about getting a cosmetology license as a way to earn money for college.

Play Your Creative Card

Teens who are looking for more than a 3 to 7 P.M. commitment might want to start their own small business in babysitting, landscaping, Web design, or graphic arts. "Get creative," says Webster. If you have a talent and find yourself using it frequently for friends and neighbors anyway, maybe it could help you earn some cash.

Greg Katz, 19, a freshman at Johns Hopkins University, went into business with his best friend when they were high school sophomores. "We wanted some extra income, but we weren't really interested in having a boss and doing it the traditional way. So we sat down and brainstormed what we could do to make money," says Katz. The duo decided to use their computer skills and launched K&R Computer Repair in North Caldwell, N.J.

They experimented with different advertising methods, from flyers to direct mailings, and built up a client list. "Any problem a person has, we can take care of it; we do upgrades, software installation, cleaning a computer virus, fixing an Internet connection," says Katz.

By identifying problems they were able to solve, Katz and his friend built a successful small business. During high school they charged $35 an hour but recently raised their rate to $50. This year they incorporated (became legally recognized as a business) and hired employees to keep the business going while they are away at college.

Katz, who is leaning toward a political science degree, hopes to keep his company going after college and well into the future. "We always felt the best option was to go into business," he says. Though starting a business was much more challenging than getting a part-time job—business owners must handle taxes and payroll, for example—he feels the payoff has been worth it. Katz and his partner have earned more money than they would have made working for an employer—and they've set the wheels in motion for their future careers.

Your Bottom Line

"The more experiences you have, the better," says Rosengart. If you don't find something you love or have a passion for right out of the gate, keep trying. Sampling a variety of jobs is a great way to jump into the work world. Don't be afraid to change your mind either. Your likes, dislikes, passions, and interests evolve as you mature, head through college, or enter adulthood, says Webster. Remember what you wanted to be at 6, 8, or 12? Chances are, you have probably changed your mind many times!

"And don't just look for jobs that pay the most money," says Webster. Everyone wants to live well and drive a cool car, but we all have talents, the potential to serve others in a positive way, and passions that we can develop even in a part-time job.

On-the-Job Tips

- *Ask questions.* You'll be surrounded by professionals with experience in their field. Talk to them about their career path during free time, advises Sharon Rosengart, director of career services at DeVry University.

- *Show initiative.* Take on as much responsibility as possible. Employers appreciate when teens go the extra mile.

- *Set goals.* Most jobs require you to get certain things done in the allotted time. Setting goals is a great way to keep on track.

- *Document your duties.* Keep a notebook and jot down the different tasks you handle on the job and the skills you've acquired. This information comes in handy when filling out future job or college applications.

- *Ask for a letter of recommendation.* If the job's been positive and you've made a meaningful contribution, ask your employer for a letter of recommendation when you leave. Use it for future jobs or for college applications.

Unconventional Job Options

If You're Into:	LOOK HERE
Animals	vet offices, zoos, pet stores, nature preserves, sanctuaries, environmental centers, rescue organizations, dog sitting/walking/grooming services
Medicine	doctor's offices, clinics, hospitals
Children	day-care centers, camps, babysitting services, tutoring, specialty classes
Health and fitness	fitness centers, healing centers, day spas, YMCAs
Outdoors	nature centers, state/national parks, town parks and recreation departments, aquariums, golf courses, country clubs, landscaping, construction
Cooking, baking	bakeries, restaurants, coffee shops, chocolatiers, cooking-supply stores, specialty food markets, delis
Art, crafts, painting, pottery	pottery shops, art/photo studios, art supply or craft stores, galleries, museums, frame shops
Cars	mechanic centers, auto-parts stores, car washes, tire retailers, custom shops

TWO

Employers Are Putting Teens at Risk

Alba Lucero Villa

According to research by the University of North Carolina on behalf of the National Institute for Occupational Safety and Health, teenagers face significant threats to safety in the workplace. These threats are due in large part to employers failing to abide by federal and state regulations regarding teen employment. In the following viewpoint writer Alba Lucero Villa cites examples from the study that highlight the dangers teens face in the workplace, such as working late hours, operating dangerous equipment, and working alone during hours that are at high risk for robberies. Villa also points out that both teens and their parents are often unaware of worker rights and federal and state regulations regarding teen employment.

Many employers are violating state and federal laws by allowing teens to operate dangerous equipment, work late hours, and perform other illegal tasks, according to the first national study of teen workers' exposure to on-the-job hazards.

The study, published in the March issue of *Pediatrics* was funded by the National Institute for Occupational Safety and Health, which has reported that each year about 230,000 teens file workers' compensation claims and another 67 die from work-related

Alba Lucero Villa, "Employers Put Teens at Risk, Study Says," *Trial*, May 2007, pp. 90–91. Reprinted by permission.

injuries. The Injury Prevention Research Center (IPRC) at the University of North Carolina conducted the study based on a 2003 telephone survey of 866 teens between 14 and 17 years old who had worked in retail and service, the largest two employment sectors for the group.

"We were particularly interested in examining violations of federal law," said Carol Runyan, lead author of the report. "What we found were fairly substantial red flags that the enforcement system isn't working."

Safety Violations

Federal regulations prohibit teens under 18 from using certain types of dangerous equipment—such as slicers, dough mixers, box crushers, or paper balers—and serving or selling alcohol. Yet the study found that 52 percent of boys and 43 percent of girls surveyed reported having performed one or more of the prohibited tasks.

"The findings show examples of employers putting profits over safety, and it's a situation that needs to be addressed," said Kenneth Margolin, a Newton, Massachusetts–based personal injury attorney who has handled workplace injury cases and written about workplace hazards.

Federal law also prohibits teens younger than 16 to work after 7 P.M. on school nights, but 37 percent of the 16-year-olds surveyed reported doing so.

"Also, we found a number of kids who are working with limited supervision or alone at night," Runyan said. "That's the time in retail where the risk is the greatest."

"Adequate training and adult supervision would seem to be a minimum amount of care owed to working teenagers," Margolin said. He noted that many teens working alone at night are "handling a lot of money without being properly trained to do what's necessary if there's a robbery."

Teen Workplace Fatalities

The study cited a 2005 Bureau of Labor Statistics (BLS) report that found that 80 teens died at their retail or service jobs between

Federal regulations prohibit teens from operating dangerous equipment. Yet one study found that 53 percent of boys and 43 percent of girls have reported performing one or more prohibited tasks.

1998 and 2002, comprising 26 percent of teen work-related fatalities. Most were homicides from robberies. The BLS report indicated that the agriculture, forestry, and fishing industries had the most teen worker deaths in that time period.

"Although teen worker fatalities are less common in the retail and service sectors than in other sectors, nonfatal injuries in these sectors are common," the IPRC study said.

"It's not a trivial problem, yet it hasn't come to the forefront of people's attention," even though most teens will have worked in at least one job by the time they graduate from high school, Runyan said.

"Parents and teens need to be more aware of their rights as workers, and employers held accountable," she added. "My hunch is that some employers know the law but haven't enforced it."

Law Reform and Enforcement

Federal regulations set the minimum requirements employers must meet when employing teen workers. Many states have supplemental laws regarding work permits and other restrictions, but the study's findings suggest widespread lack of enforcement, Runyan said. She called on state labor departments to step up oversight and highlighted Massachusetts's recent reform efforts.

Massachusetts updated its child labor laws in January [2007], requiring work permits for all minors—previously only 14- and 15-year-olds needed them—and mandating direct supervision for minors working after 8 P.M. to reduce their vulnerability to crime and injuries. The new law also authorized the state attorney general to fine employers who violate child labor laws.

Margolin called the changes in his state a major step in the right direction, but cautioned that reform works only if a good law is backed with proper enforcement and adequate community education.

Teen workers in Massachusetts are injured at about twice the rate of adults, and six have been killed at work in the last seven years—most doing jobs that were prohibited under the state's child labor laws, according to the nonprofit Massachusetts Coalition for Occupational Safety and Health. Yet, not one of their employers has been prosecuted for the violations that resulted in deaths, according to the organization.

Further Research

Runyan and her research team conducted a parallel study with the surveyed teens' parents to gauge their level of involvement in

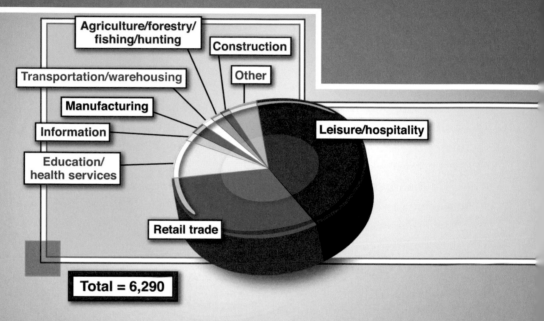

Work-Related Injuries and Illnesses Among Under-18 Employees, 2007

These data reported by employers are for injuries requiring at least one day away from work. These data do not include youth who work on small farms, youth who work for government agencies, or youth who are self-employed.

Agriculture/forestry/fishing/hunting

Construction

Other

Transportation/warehousing

Manufacturing

Information

Leisure/hospitality

Education/health services

Retail trade

Total = 6,290

Taken from: "Selected Charts on Young Worker Employment, Injuries and Illnesses," Centers for Disease Control and Prevention (CDC)/National Institute for Occupational Safety and Health (NIOSH). www.cdc.gov/niosh/topics/youth/chtpkgfig10.html.

their children's work and knowledge of current child labor laws. That study, which will be published in a few months, found that parents aren't as aware of what their teens are doing at work as they should be, but they want to learn more, Runyan said.

The research team is also in the process of conducting a comparative study of Canadian teen workers. While Canada does not have the work permit laws that 41 U.S. states have or a federal law that resembles the Fair Labor Standards Act, Runyan said, its government pays "a fair amount of attention to worker safety."

THREE

Teens Can Take Measures to Protect Themselves at Work

Melissa Daly

> While every year teens are injured and even killed at work or from work-sustained injuries, they can also take measures to lessen the risks. Melissa Daly, a writer for *Career World*, a magazine for middle and high school students, discusses the dangers specific to several types of teen employment: restaurant jobs, retail jobs, outdoor jobs, and heavy-machinery jobs. Daly also presents warnings that will help teens stay safe at particular types of jobs, strategies that will help them stay safe in any job, and websites where teens can look up information to learn about their workplace rights under the specific laws that have been put into place to keep them safe.

There's no doubt about it: Working during the summer always beats sitting around. You get to meet new people, bond with your crew after hours, add a line to your resume, and maybe even learn a new skill. The whole time, you're earning money to spend or save for whatever you want. The catch: Working puts you in a new environment that comes with its own set of health hazards.

"Young workers may not believe that some of these hazards—such as sun exposure, accidents, or even crime—will ever affect them. But they can, if precautionary steps aren't taken," says

Melissa Daly, "Risky Business: Here's How to Stay Out of Harm's Way on the Job This Summer," *Career World*, a Weekly Reader Publication, April 2008, pp. 20–23. Reprinted by permission.

Robert Nester, a registered nurse and health scientist at the Occupational Safety and Health Administration (OSHA). About 70 teens die each year of work-related injuries, and tens of thousands visit emergency rooms. Whatever your dream summer job is, here's what to look out for to stay safe.

Restaurant Jobs

From drive-throughs to five-star restaurants, food service is a big industry for teen workers. You could get a job as a host, waitperson, cook, barista, dishwasher, or cashier. With all the hot pans, food spills, and knives lurking about, those aren't always the safest gigs, though. "The main concerns here are burns and slip-and-fall injuries," notes Elise Handelman, director of the Office of Occupational Health Nursing at OSHA.

You can do plenty to avoid getting hurt, however. "At the seafood restaurant where I'm a hostess and busser, I have to walk in the kitchen after they've just sprayed down the floors each night. So my supervisor told me where to buy nonslip shoes," says Courtney, 19, of Summerfield, Fla.

Here are your top priorities for staying safe at a restaurant job:

- Slow down. Safety is more important than speed, even when customers (or your boss!) seem impatient.
- Avoid falls. Wear covered, nonslip shoes and clean up any spills immediately.
- Think "hot." Assume machines, plates, and surfaces—as well as oil, steam, and food—are hot, even if you're not sure. Use dry cloths to carry hot dishes, wear long-sleeved cotton clothes when cooking, and always use tongs rather than your hands when you need to handle hot equipment or food.

Retail Jobs

Folding clothes, stocking shelves, or running a cash register may not seem very dangerous, but retail jobs actually cause the highest number of deaths among young workers aside from farm jobs, mainly because of crimes committed at grocery, convenience, jewelry, and other types of stores. "I'm never alone in the store,"

Distribution of young workers by industry, 2009

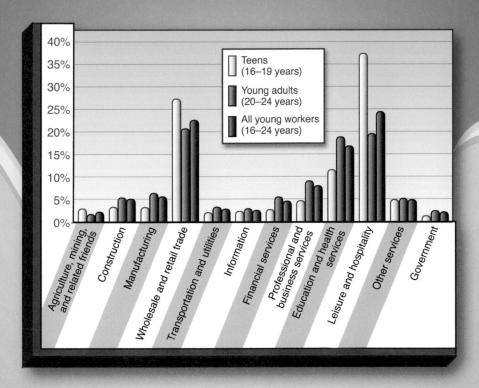

Legend:
- Teens (16–19 years)
- Young adults (20–24 years)
- All young workers (16–24 years)

Industries:
- Agriculture, mining, and related friends
- Construction
- Manufacturing
- Wholesale and retail trade
- Transportation and utilities
- Information
- Financial services
- Professional and business services
- Education and health services
- Leisure and hospitality
- Other services
- Government

Taken from: "Understanding the Economy: Unemployment Among Young Workers," US Congress Joint Economic Committee, May 2010.

says Evelyn, 18, who works at a shoe store in Manhattan, "but I do have to leave at 10:30 some nights, and I worry about getting home safely." She keeps her cell phone at the ready, sometimes with 911 punched in so she can react more quickly in case of an emergency. "Violence is a major concern," confirms Handelman. "But so are more common injuries like back strains due to heavy lifting."

How to protect yourself:

- Never work alone, especially at night. Always stay within sight of at least one coworker.

Teens Can Take Measures to Protect Themselves at Work   23

- Protect your back. To avoid back strain, wear a weight belt for any heavy lifting, and use a hand truck instead of carrying large or awkward loads. Make several trips instead of trying to carry everything at once.
- Know how to handle a tough situation. Be sure you receive training from your employer on how to deal with a robbery attempt or even just an angry customer. If a robbery occurs, hand over whatever money or merchandise the thief wants and don't leave the store, either with the thief or to follow him or her. No amount of property is worth risking your life for.

Outdoor Jobs

Working as a lifeguard, a camp counselor, or an amusement park employee can be a ton of fun, as long as you watch out for a few health-related issues. "When exposed to the elements, you want to be careful of communicable diseases, sunburn, and heat exhaustion and dehydration," cautions Handelman. Andrew, a 17-year-old lifeguard in McLean, Va., agrees. "One week, I worked several long shifts during the hottest part of the day, and I got dehydrated," says Andrew. "After that, I made sure to drink lots of water and wear a shirt to protect my body from the sun."

Your stay-healthy checklist for any outdoor job:
- Be sun safe. Every day, wear a broad-spectrum SPF 15 sunscreen, a wide-brimmed hat, and sunglasses labeled "100% UV protection."
- Drink plenty of fluids. Plenty means 16 to 32 ounces of water, juice, or a sports drink per hour when you're active in hot weather.
- Sweat it. If you experience heavy sweating or no sweating at all, especially red or especially pale skin, dizziness, nausea, headache, weakness, or confusion, tell someone immediately—you may have heat exhaustion or heat stroke, which can be fatal. Cool down with shade, rest, a cool bath, and/or air conditioning.
- Protect yourself from communicable diseases. Wear insect repellent and protective clothing to ward off mosquitoes,

which can carry the potentially fatal West Nile virus, and ticks, which can cause Lyme disease. Ask your doctor if you're up to date on booster shots, such as the one for tetanus— transmitted through cuts and puncture wounds—which you need to get every 10 years.

Heavy-Machinery Jobs

Landscaping, farming, and construction jobs can be great money-makers, but think twice before you accept one. "Many are illegal for workers under the age of 18," says Handelman. Because of all the power-driven machinery and opportunities to be struck by

Teens are prohibited from working in jobs that involve operating power-driven machinery because of the danger of being caught in or struck by heavy equipment, yet farming jobs are not prohibited.

or caught between vehicles or other heavy objects, those lines of work are considered especially dangerous; however, not all are off-limits. "I work for a home improvement company, getting tools for my supervisor and performing basic plumbing tasks," says Bobby, 17, of Owings, Md. "If we're doing anything that produces dust, we wear dust masks; when handling sharp objects, we wear gloves; and when using things like nail guns, we wear eye protection."

Whatever your specific responsibilities are, keep yourself out of harm's way:

- Know your limits. Know which tasks you are and aren't allowed to perform—see "For More [Information]."
- Stay alert at all times. Get plenty of sleep before each work-day, and always wear all the protective gear your employer requires, even if you don't think you'll need it.
- Protect your ears. If you have to shout to be heard by someone next to you while on the job, you may be suffering hearing damage, which is untreatable and permanent. Your employer must provide hearing protection even if you're not the one operating the loud machine. (By the way, noise levels at jobs in places like music stores or amusement parks can also be harmful—if your workplace fails the shouting test, wear earplugs if possible.)

For More Information

Your employer is required by law to provide a safe workplace, no matter what your age. If you think your job may be putting you at risk, don't hesitate to tell your supervisor, your parents, or both. You can also call 1-800-321-OSHA (6742) for answers to your questions. For more information, check out the following sites.

- *Teen Workers*: The tips here are just a starting point; get more detailed advice for almost any teen job here: www.osha.gov/SLTg/teenworkers
- *elaws: Prohibited Occupations*: Some jobs—such as those involving construction tools, farm implements, or food-service machinery—are considered to be too dangerous for teens. www.dol.gov/elaws/esa/flsa/docs/hazardous.asp
- *elaws: Hours Restrictions*: Find out what hours you're allowed to work. www.dol.gov/elaws/esa/flsa/docs/hours.asp

FOUR

Sexual Harassment of Teens at Work Is Increasing

Jill Schachner Chanen

> One of the hazards that teens face at work is sexual harassment. While media attention and training requirements have shed light on this issue in recent decades, sexual harassment claims have increased among the teen workforce. Jill Schachner Chanen, a lawyer and assistant managing editor of the *ABA Journal* (American Bar Association), writes about this trend in the following viewpoint. As well as presenting statistics, she theorizes about reasons for this trend, briefly discusses the major relevant court cases, and presents suggestions to employers that could protect teens, such as making written policies easier to understand and printing toll-free numbers on paychecks that employees can call to report harassment.

When it comes to sexual harassment, lawyers have done a thorough job educating adult workers about the limits of acceptable behavior in the workplace. The same can't be said of the youth workforce, however, as studies have shown an increase in sexual harassment claims.

Employment lawyers say suits by teen workers could become a major liability for businesses, and several recent court decisions involving teenage sexual harassment in the workplace attest to that.

Jill Schachner Chanen, "New Troubles for Teens at Work: With More Youths on the Job, Sex Harassment Claims Are on the Rise," *ABA Journal 94*, April 2008, pp. 22–23. Reprinted by permission.

"Really obvious sexual harassment [among adults] is declining," says Jennifer A. Drobac, a law professor at Indiana University in Indianapolis who studies sex harassment and has written a legal textbook on the subject. "The problem with teens is that they don't know right from wrong. They don't know what is acceptable workplace behavior. Teens don't get the training. They don't read the manuals."

While most American businesses have anti-harassment policies, procedures and training programs firmly in place for their adult workers, teenage workers often fall through the cracks. They tend to be part-time, temporary or seasonal. And in workplaces that commonly employ teens—fast-food restaurants, movie theaters and retail stores—managers also often are teenagers.

"It's a line-management issue," says Boston employment lawyer Jaclyn Kugell, a partner at Morgan, Brown & Joy. "Employers that implement these preventive measures should ensure that all managers, regardless of their age, are aware of the rules."

A Trend Taking Shape

According to Drobac's research, teen sexual harassment cases filed with the Equal Employment Opportunity Commission [EEOC] have risen from 2 percent of all cases in 2001 to 8 percent in 2004. Over that period the number of all cases filed declined, from 15,475 to 13,136, according to the EEOC. Though Drobac has not been able to obtain updated statistics from government agencies, she expects the numbers to continue to rise.

Referring to 16- to 19-year-olds, the EEOC "has seen, through charges filed and anecdotal evidence, that discrimination is a problem for many in this group," according to the commission's fiscal year 2007 performance budget.

More than 7.1 million young adults ages 16 to 19 were employed during the summer of 2004, according to the report. Between 33 percent and 44 percent of teens 16 to 19 worked during the school year from 2001 to 2006.

Research conducted at the University of Southern Maine in 2002 further underscores the potential for liability. According to

To reduce the incidence of sexual harassment of teens, policies and procedures must be understandable to the workforce and to employers.

professor of social work Susan Fineran, 35 percent of some 300 high school students surveyed said they were subjected to sexual harassment at work; more than 60 percent of the harassed respondents were teenage girls.

Teens View Jobs Differently

"There is a different story with teenagers," says Memphis, Tenn., employment lawyer Jim Mulroy, a partner at Kiesewetter Wise Kaplan Prather. "Most of these are part-time jobs and are not the central focus of their life as it is for an adult. There is lots of playing around and socializing at work. They don't differentiate the workplace from what they do at school or at the YMCA or at

Ten Largest Settlements in Bias Complaints Against Restaurants

Defendant	EEOC* Office	Complaint	Amount
1). Valentino Las Vegas	Los Angeles, CA	Sexual harassment	$600,000
2). Wendy's	Charlotte, NC	Sexual harassment	$487,500
3). JB's	Phoenix, AZ	Sexual harassment	$435,000
4). Midamerica/Burger King	St. Louis, MO	Sexual harassment	$400,000
5). Colonial Ice Cream	Chicago, IL	Sexual harassment	$386,000
6). Pizza Hut of America	Los Angeles, CA	Sexual harassment	$360,000
7). Pizza of Florida/ ABC Pizza	Miami, FL	Sexual harassment	$325,000
8). Outback Steakhouse	Miami, FL	Sexual harassment	$305,000
9). Jack in the Box	San Francisco, CA	Sexual harassment	$300,000
10). Canyon Lake Country Club	Los Angeles, CA	Sexual harassment	$285,000

* Equal Employment Opportunity Commission

Taken from: Dina Berta, "EEOC: Industry Sued Most in Claims of Teen Harassment," *Nation's Restaurant News*, February 5, 2007, pp. 48–49.

a dance. They have a tendency not to care about those kinds of rules unless it is made important by their employer."

Because of their informal, festive ambience, restaurants are particularly vulnerable. According to a 2007 article in the industry publication *Nation's Restaurant News*, 72 of 127 EEOC complaints involving teens dating back to 1999 were against restaurant companies, whether independent operators or chains and franchisees.

All but 11 of the 72 complaints were based on sexual harassment charges. And restaurants paid out more than $7.3 million to settle sexual harassment lawsuits involving teenage workers.

Beyond Policies and Procedures

In a November [2007] decision, the Chicago-based 7th U.S. Circuit Court of Appeals put the business community on notice that it is no longer enough simply to have a policy and reporting procedure in place. (*EEOC v. V&J Foods.*)

Writing for the court, Judge Richard Posner warned businesses that they need to go beyond the standard set by the U.S. Supreme Court in two 1998 companion cases, *Faragher v. City of Boca Raton* and *Burlington Industries v. Ellerth*, to avoid liability in teenage sexual harassment claims. Those two cases set rules for determining when an employer will be liable for sexual harassment committed by its supervisors. They also spelled out a defense that employers can raise in certain circumstances.

Sexual harassment policies and procedures must be written so as to be meaningful and understandable to the workforce, says Dallas lawyer Michael Maslanka, a partner in Ford & Harrison, a national labor and employment firm.

The V&J Foods case arose after a teenage employee of a Burger King franchise in Milwaukee claimed that her manager repeatedly subjected her to unwanted sexual advances. Though the teen repeatedly complained to restaurant managers, her complaints eventually came back to her harasser-manager, who eventually fired her.

"An employer is not required to tailor its complaint procedures to the competence of each individual employee," Posner wrote. "But it is part of V&J's business plan to employ teenagers, part-time workers often working for the first time. Knowing that it has many teenage employees, the company was obligated to suit its procedures to the understanding of the average teenager."

The 7th Circuit decision is significant "because it says one size does not fit all" when it comes to sexual harassment policies, says Maslanka. "You have to look at the people in your workforce and make sure that the message is understandable to them. It's not that the vice president of human resources sitting in the Sears Tower understands; it is whether the teen understands it."

More to Consider

V&J Foods comes on the heels of a 2006 teen sex harassment case, *Doe v. Oberweis Dairy*, in which the 7th Circuit held that a minor's consent to sex does not operate as a complete bar to a Title VII[1] sexual harassment case. Courts instead have to look to age of consent laws when determining whether consent to sexual activity will have legal weight.

Further, wrote Posner in *Oberweis Dairy*, "an employer of teenagers is not in loco parentis, but he acts at his peril if he fails to warn their parents when he knows or should know that their children are at substantial risk of statutory rape by an older, male shift supervisor in circumstances constituting workplace harassment."

Because there is no consistency among the states as to the age of consent, businesses will need to craft policies that will work in every state where they operate, Drobac says.

Drobac notes that, in addition to the 7th Circuit cases, the EEOC entered into a consent decree in 2006 with Taco Bell Corp., requiring the fast-food chain to adopt and implement a training program with special emphasis on workplace issues that affect youth workers. The decree is unpublished, she says.

Better Protection

Taken together, employment lawyers say, these cases should provide more protections for the teenage workforce.

Many employment lawyers say they are already advising clients to take a second look at their harassment policies and procedures. Maslanka is rewriting policies to put the onus [responsibility] on employees to keep complaining if they do not get an adequate response the first or second time they complain about harass-

---

1. Part of the Civil Rights Act of 1964, Title VII prohibits workplace discrimination or harassment based on race, color, religion, national origin, or sex.

ment. Mulroy has seen a client print on paychecks the toll-free number that employees can call to complain about harassment at any time of the day.

Despite such efforts, other lawyers emphasize that employers need to remember the context of a teenage employee-manager's life. "They are likely socializing with their peers in school in a way that is different from how we as adults interact with our peers at work. Then, they go to the workplace and are expected to adhere to standards of behavior that may not have applied so strictly only three hours before," says Kugell.

"We are asking a lot of this younger work group, particularly if we don't clearly explain both the standards of behavior that apply in the workplace and the consequences for violating them."

FIVE

Parental Involvement Makes Managing This Generation of Teens Challenging

Neil Howe and William Strauss

In 2000 the first wave of a new generation—the millennials, sometimes grouped with those known as generation Y—graduated from high school and entered the adult workforce. Defined by the authors of this viewpoint as those born between 1982 and 2001, this generation constitutes an increasing percentage of today's adult workforce and makes up the entire population of the current teen workforce. In the following viewpoint Neil Howe and William Strauss, strategic planning consultants and coauthors of four books on generational differences, discuss one particular challenge of managing this generation: the overinvolvement of their baby boomer and generation X parents. Described as "helicopter parents," they have been known to submit resumes for their children, accompany them to interviews, and help them with work projects. Howe and Strauss explain the defining characteristics of these parents and their children and trace the social factors responsible. Additionally, they cite statistics that describe the extent of parental involvement and their children's reactions.

Neil Howe and William Strauss, "Helicopter Parents in the Workplace," Talent 2.0, November 2007, pp. 4–6. Reprinted by permission.

Like all American generations that came before, Millennials have been uniquely shaped by the era in which its members grew up and came of age, and that formative influence has had enduring effects.

Many of the grandparents of today's young workers are members of the Silent Generation (now mostly in retirement). They were children during the crisis years of the Great Depression and World War II, and defined youth during the "golden age" of the 1940s and '50s. They entered the workplace during the postwar era when returning veterans were given top priority (well-captured in the film "The Best Years of Our Lives"). They were expected to be, and they were "organization men."

Many of the parents of today's young workers are Boomers. Members of this argumentative and values-obsessed generation (today squarely in midlife) were children during an era of postwar complacency. They defined youth in the 1960s and 1970s; an era of social turmoil, youth anger, and steeply worsening youth trends (such as rising crime rates and substance abuse, and falling academic achievement). They entered the workplace at the height of the Consciousness Revolution, as arguments between the young and old reached a fevered pitch and workplace productivity began to decline.

Millennials' older siblings and younger parents are part of Generation X. These pragmatists and survivalists were children during the Consciousness Revolution. They defined youth during the 1980s and early 1990s, and became the young workers of the dot com bubble, an individualistic era of market-driven free agency.

Millennials as Children

Likewise, the Millennial Generation has its own place in history. Recall the last quarter century of American family life. The greatest change came in 1982. The February 22, 1982 issue of *Time* offered a cover story about an array of thirty-something Boomers choosing (finally) to become moms and dads. That same year, bright yellow "Baby on Board" signs began popping up in station-wagon windows. During the Gen Xer childhood, planned parenting meant contraceptives; suddenly it meant visits to the fertility clinic. *The era of the wanted baby had begun.*

In September 1982, the first Tylenol scare led to parental panic over trick-or-treating—Halloween suddenly found itself encased in hotlines, advisories, and statutes—a fate that would soon befall many other once-innocent child pastimes, from bicycle-riding to BB guns. A few months later came national hysteria over the sexual abuse of toddlers, leading to dozens of adult convictions after what skeptics will liken to Salem-style trials. All the while, new books (*The Disappearance of Childhood, Children Without Childhood, Our Endangered Children*) assailed the "anything goes" parental treatment of children since the mid-1960s. *The era of the protected toddler had begun.*

Through the early 1980s, the national rates for many behaviors damaging to children—divorce, abortion, violent crime, alcohol and drug abuse—reached their postwar high-water mark. The well-being of children began to dominate the national debate over family issues. In 1983, the federal Nation at Risk report on education blasted grade-school students as "a rising tide of mediocrity," prompting editorialists to implore teachers and adults to do better by America's next batch of kids. In 1984, "Children of the Corn" and "Firestarter" failed at the box office. These were merely the latest installments in a child-horror film genre that had been popular and profitable for well over a decade, ever since "Rosemary's Baby" and "The Exorcist." But parents were beginning to prefer a new kind of movie ("Baby Boom," "Parenthood," "Three Men and a Baby") about wonderful babies and adults who improve their lives by looking after them. *The era of the worthy child had begun.*

Millennials as Teens

In 1990, the *Wall Street Journal* and *New York Times* had headlines— "The '60s Generation, Once High on Drugs, Warns Its Children" and "Do As I Say, Not As I Did." Polls showed that Boomer parents did not want their own children to have the same freedom with drugs, alcohol, and sex that they once enjoyed.

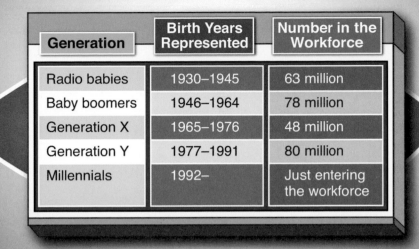

Generations in the Workforce

Generation	Birth Years Represented	Number in the Workforce
Radio babies	1930–1945	63 million
Baby boomers	1946–1964	78 million
Generation X	1965–1976	48 million
Generation Y	1977–1991	80 million
Millennials	1992–	Just entering the workforce

Taken from: Karen E. Klein, "Managing Across the Generation Gap," *Bloomberg Business Week*, February 12, 2007.

Between 1986 and 1991, the number of periodicals offered to young children doubled. In tot-TV fare, "Barney and Friends" (featuring teamwork and what kids share in common) stole the limelight from "Sesame Street" (featuring individualism and what makes each kid unique). During 1996, major-party nominees [Bob] Dole and [Bill] Clinton dueled for the presidency in a campaign full of talk about the middle-school offspring of "soccer moms." The next year, Millennials began to make an impression on pop culture. Thanks to the Spice Girls, Hanson, and others, 1997 ushered in a whole new musical sound—happier, brighter, and more innocent. *The era of the perfected teen had begun.*

Through the late 1990s, these same much-watched youths passed through high school, accompanied by enormous parental, educational, and media fascination. After the April 1999 Columbine tragedy was replayed again and again on the news, this adult absorption with Millennial safety, achievement, and morality reached a fever pitch. Teen employment declined, in part because it was perceived as less useful than other ways of building resumés and careers. Young people began to spend less time flipping burgers and more time doing homework, and new industries emerged offering resumé-enhancing summer experiences other than paid employment.

Millennials as Adults

By the year 2000, Millennials began graduating from high school and entering the workplace, the armed forces, and colleges. Colleges began to feel the glare of the media and a level of parental involvement that college administrators had never seen. By the middle 2000s the term "helicopter parent" was in wide use on campuses. In the spring of 2002, the first Millennials received Associate degrees, and increasingly entered trades and service fields. At the same time, internships started to rise both in numbers and importance, as Millennials in 4-year degree programs looked ahead to their future employment. In 2003–04, Millennials met with recruiters, wrote resumés, graduated from college and entered the workplace in full force. Employers began noticing something new, from a focus on long-term job security to a desire for constant feedback, to comfort with teamwork, to hovering parents. *The era of the obsessively-coached young worker had begun.*

In 2006 and 2007, Millennials started graduating from business and law schools. The glare of the media turned to student loan controversies as the pressure of student loans began bearing down on this generation of young graduates. More and more media and corporate attention focused on youth culture in the workplace, from young adult surveys to articles on workplace attire to special training workshops on how to manage today's young employees.

What Are Parents Doing?

Highly involved parents have followed Millennials through every stage of life, attending "mommy and me" pre-school classes, challenging poor grades, negotiating with coaches, and helping their children register for college classes, and choose among prospective employers. Now, a rising tide of parents are hovering over their twenty-something children's job search and early employment, contacting employers to complain, cajole, and promote their son or daughter.

Employers report a wide variety of parental involvement. "Most of the stuff parents do is benign," says Phil Gardner, director of [a 2007] Michigan State [University] study, but most employers see parents as intrusions.

Parents who get involved most often gather information about prospective employers: Fully 40% of employers have had parents gather employment information for their children. Nearly one-third of employers have seen parents submit a resumé on their child's behalf, prompting one manager to comment: "Please tell

Many baby boomer and Generation X parents have been known to submit resumes for their children and to accompany them to job interviews.

your child that you have submitted a resumé to a company. We have called a student from our resumé pool only to find they did not know anything about our company and were not interested in a position with us." Over one quarter of employers have had parents promote their children for a position, and 15% have had parents call to complain if the company does not hire their son or daughter.

A smaller share of employers report even more hands-on parental involvement, including negotiating salary and benefits (seen by 9% of employers), advocating for salary increases (seen by 6%), and actually attending the interview (seen by 4%).

Commonly, young workers get help from their parents to complete work assignments by a deadline, or have parents review their work and make improvements, report employers. Employers have also witnessed a number of employees who insist on talking to their parents before meeting with a supervisor who is reprimanding or disciplining them.

Employers report that fathers are more likely than mothers to get involved in negotiations when a son or daughter is not hired or is being disciplined by an employer. Mothers, on the other hand, are more likely to collect information on the company and arrange for company visits and interviews.

Some young hires feel their parents take hovering too far. A 2006 online poll of 400 students and young adults by career website Experience Inc. found 25% said their parents were "overly involved to the point that their involvement was either annoying or embarrassing." Yet employers acknowledge that, for the most part, this generation expects and welcomes parental involvement more than older generations did at the same age.

SIX

Teen Employees Should Not Be Judged by Their Generation

Steve Carlson

> Steve Carlson, a researcher of assessment tools used to hire, manage, and coach employees, is critical of attempts by journalists and other writers to label people by their generations—baby boomers, generation X, or generation Y, for example. In this viewpoint, first published in *Supervision* magazine, he shows that many writers do not agree on generational titles, timelines, or characteristics and points out that most writers do not use solid research to support their theories regarding generational differences. He also cites research indicating that older and younger workers share similar values, although they may express their values differently, and that individuals in any given generation are diverse.

Supervisors from all types of organizations are grappling with the influx of new, younger employees into the workforce. In response to this situation, numerous books and articles in trade publications have attempted to name, define, and shed light on what behavioral characteristics this newest generation presumably exhibits. Some writers attempt to instruct supervisors on how to use generational characteristics to motivate and manage individuals born between certain years. Even a quick read through

Steve Carlson, "Managing Gen-Y: Supervising the Person, not the Generation," *Supervision*, February 1, 2010, pp. 9–11. Reprinted by permission.

Though individuals of any given generation are diverse, studies indicate that older and younger workers share similar values.

these articles shows how murky the definitions and descriptions are of this newest generation. Some call it "Gen-Y" because the people born in it came after the so-called "X-Generation." Others name these individuals "Millennials" because of the proximity of their birth to the year 2000. Additional titles included in this confusing mix are "Gen Why?," "Internet Generation," "Gen Next," "MyPod Generation," "Baby Boomlets," "Echo Boomers," "Boomerang Generation," "Generation Now," and "Generation Waking Up."

An Imprecise Definition

Defining who fits within this generation is equally imprecise, and depends upon the writer. Traditionally, the amount of time between generations is about 30 years and is "accepted as the average period between the birth of parents and the birth of their offspring." Writers on the subject of Gen-Y do not necessarily follow this definition. One, for example, defines Gen-Y as those people born during a fifteen year period between the very late 1970s and the mid 1990s. Another extends it to a 20 year period between the start of the 1980s and the beginning of the new millennium.

A Broad Range of Characteristics

The behavioral characteristics of the generation are also wide-ranging. Some writers suggest that Gen-Y is "optimistic," "cautious," "realistic," and having "diversification expectations." Others suggest that it wants to "heal the planet," while being "ambitious," "loyal," "wanting a quest," and being "networkers by nature." Supervisors must be diligent to look behind the rhetoric of many of these books and articles. While some articles do reference hard data, there seems to be a fair amount of sweeping generalizations made with few referencing citations beyond the author's perceptions and observations.

Research Reveals Similar Values

One researcher who has actually collected and analyzed hard data is Dr. Jennifer Deal of the Center for Creative Leadership in her book *Retiring the Generation Gap: How Employees Young & Old Can Find Common Ground*. She researched groups of people comprising multiple generations. Her research focused on how the individuals from different generations answered questions differently based upon their generational perceptions. She came to some interesting conclusions about the perceived values individuals of different generations possess. Her research indicated that the values between older and younger workers were not substantially different. Instead, the issue usually had to do with how individuals demonstrated those values. The only way to understand the expression of values is to engage employees in order to promote true understanding. Deal concludes her book stating, "When you see a conflict that others identify as being caused by the generation gap, you know that you need to look deeper for the real causes of the conflict."

While it is laudable that supervisors are looking for new ways to manage young people entering the work force, caution should be applied in managing such employees based predominantly upon when they were born in history. It is reasonable to assume that younger people would tend to be more adept than those in older generations at something like social networking, texting, or video conferencing. Undoubtedly, young people comprise a large bulk of participants in social media sites. Certainly those individuals currently in their late teens and twenties were influenced by a globalized, Post-9/11 world. Such an environment is bound to have an effect on younger individuals growing up in it. While one can reasonably make the case that younger people tend to pick up on the newest technological advances and may be influenced by economic globalization, it is another thing to develop a generational profile based upon those assertions.

Any Generation Is Too Diverse to Generalize

The United States is a very diverse country and however the Gen-Y is defined, it is a massive grouping of individuals coming from vastly different cultural, geographic, socio-economic, ethnic, and educational backgrounds. How can anyone make truly meaningful generalizations about the management of people from such a diverse population? Consider the response authors would receive if they wrote about how to motivate or manage individuals

Percentage saying there are "very strong/strong" conflicts between . . .

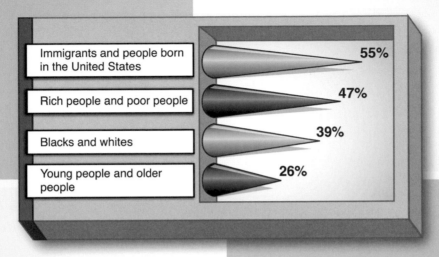

Immigrants and people born in the United States	55%
Rich people and poor people	47%
Blacks and whites	39%
Young people and older people	26%

Taken from: Paul Taylor and Richard Morin, "Forty Years after Woodstock: A Gentler Generation Gap," Pew Research Center, August 12, 2009. http://pwesocialtrends.org/pubs/739/woodstock-gentler-generation-gap-music-by-age.

from a particular ethnicity/race. Such writers would be scorned, and reasonably so. Simply because people are from the same generation does not automatically mean they will all share the same generational characteristics.

Employees Are Unique Individuals

Over the years, our research at PDP, Inc has shown that, regardless of the generation in which people are born, they have their own unique set of behavioral characteristics and motivators. A supervisor may have a team of four Gen-Y employees. If he takes the effort, he just might find that his employees from the same generation have vastly different characteristics. Onc employee might be described as "direct and driven," a second be accurately described as "dependable and stable," still another who is "accurate and detailed," and the fourth one who prides herself on being "persuasive and influential." While all these employees may be extremely tech savvy, knowing how to load an iPod, tweet their thoughts to the world, or text a mile-a-minute, they are not all motivated by the same things. Nor will they respond identically if they are managed simply based upon how their generation is supposed to act. In fact, how individuals leverage their technological skills has everything to do with the characteristics that make up who they are. Gen-Y should not be viewed solely as a monolith with specific characteristics, but as a group of unique individuals engaging and being influenced by an increasingly globalized society.

Set Clear Performance Standards

How does a supervisor make use of this kind of information in her actual work setting? How does she understand the motivators and characteristics of her younger employees? The answer is not as hard as it might seem. Instead of relying upon ideas of what a stereotypical "GenY-er" wants, the manager needs to engage the actual employees she has. This is done by managing performance. The supervisor sits down briefly with her younger employees to clearly outline her expectations of them for the coming months. She outlines the competency factors required for success in the employee's unique position and how performance will be measured. Specific behaviors relating to particular tasks should be clearly described.

Discover Motivators

The supervisor then works with her employees to determine what their unique motivators are and how as the manager she can express them in a way that fits within their values. She could simply ask a question like, "Describe what is or would be most motivating to you in your present situation (e.g. 'harmony' or 'taking risks')." She asks her employees to determine three or four of these motivators and define what they mean within the position. There are also reporting mechanisms the manager can provide to her employees to use to simply check off different motivators.

With both the manager's expectations and employee's motivators all known up-front, the supervisor can better manager her employees on a day-to-day basis. Because of the mutual understanding that is developed between a younger employee and the supervisor, there will be no surprises when it comes time to provide feedback or performance appraisal to her employees.

Supervision and management have always been hard work. Using a generational profile approach to motivating younger workers may sound like a great short cut to understanding employees, particularly given the amount of recent articles written about the subject. However, caution must be exercised in how supervisors generalize the characteristics of their younger employees. No matter how much we want to generalize, young people are still individuals with different motivators. Effective management will always require great effort. That is why good managers continue to be such a great asset to organizations of every kind.

SEVEN

Teen Unemployment Is at a Record High

Emily C. Dooley

> With teen unemployment at its highest level since World War II, writer Emily C. Dooley, in an article for the *Richmond Times-Dispatch*, a Virginia newspaper, examines the reasons for this trend. She explains that more retirees are being forced to work, more unemployed adults are taking lower-wage jobs, and new college graduates are biding their time until a job in their field opens up—circumstances that collectively squeeze teens out of the job market. Teens from low-income families are even harder hit because there are fewer major retailers in low-income areas, and obtaining transportation to jobs outside their neighborhoods can be difficult and expensive.

Ask Clifton Price where he would be without job training and the teen sums it up in a word.

"Lost."

The junior at John Marshall High School in Richmond [Virginia] applied unsuccessfully several times for jobs at local supermarkets and retail stores.

Sometimes prospective employers said they would be in touch but never called. Other times they said he wasn't old enough. "It was hard," he said.

Emily C. Dooley, "Teens Dig for Jobs: It's a Tough Job Market This Year, with Many Contributing Factors," *Richmond (VA) Times-Dispatch*, May 4, 2008. Reprinted by permission.

For teens looking for work this summer [2008], the outlook nationally appears bleak. Locally it's a mixed bag.

Nationwide, the percentage of teens working this summer is expected to be at the lowest level since the end of World War II, said Andrew Sum, a professor and director of the Center for Labor Market Studies at Northeastern University.

About 34 percent of all teens between ages 16 and 19 will have a job this summer, down from 45 percent in 2000, Sum's research found.

Forty-nine percent of hiring managers representing hourly employers, such as retailers and restaurants where many teens work, do not plan to take on new seasonal workers in 2008, according to a study commissioned by SnagAJob.com, the Henrico County–based job Web site that caters to hourly and part-time workers.

Multiple Factors

The causes of the slump in teen hiring are many—a slowing economy, retirees coming back into the market, college students taking hourly jobs as they search for career-path employment.

When the economy is in a recession, teens tend to be the ones to lose jobs first, according to a report by the Bureau of Labor Statistics.

Those with little or no work experience tend to have a harder time finding jobs.

"It's going to be a crazy summer if we don't get these kids on the path to getting job skills," said Todd Elliott, program director for the Northside Youth Initiative, which operates a career program for those between ages 14 and 24.

While Sum predicted a harsh national outlook, an economist with the Virginia Employment Commission thinks the state will fare better.

One reason is that the tourism and hospitality industries employ a lot of teens, said William F. Mezger, the commission's chief economist.

Young Workers Face High Levels of Unemployment

Shaded vertical areas indicate recessions, as classified by the National Bureau of Economic Research.

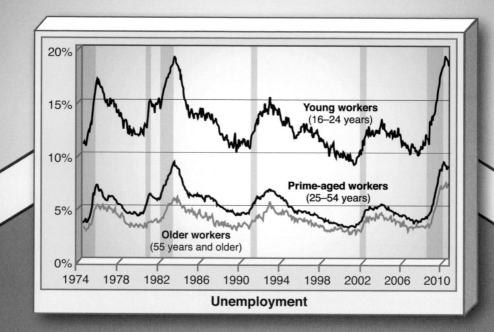

Unemployment

Taken from: "Understanding the Economy: Unemployment Among Young Workers," US Congress Joint Economic Committee, May 2010.

Kings Dominion, for instance, hires about 900 teens during the season. The northern Hanover County theme park employs a total of between 2,500 and 3,000 people seasonally each year, and the number of applicants and workers has remained steady in recent years.

Tre Brown, 17, from Highland Springs, landed a job at the park last year and was rehired this year as a sales associate who entertains guests as they compete for prizes at carnival games.

"It helps me pay for anything I want," he said. "Gas money, lunch money and anything I want to spend my money on." . . .

Socioeconomic Disadvantages

Income and race sometimes play a factor in teen employment.

Teens from higher-income families tend to have cars and live near malls in suburban areas where there are retail opportunities. They also often have working parents who can help them get a job or provide tips on how to land employment, Sum said.

But black teens from low-income families making less than $20,000 face a more dire reality. In 2007, 19 percent of black teens seeking employment had a job, while 36 percent of low-income white teens ages 16–19 found employment, his research found.

In low-income areas, there aren't as many jobs in the neighborhoods and parents often don't work or have less ability to help their children enter the job market, the researcher said.

The issue hits Richmond, where 18.5 percent of residents in 2005 lived in poverty, according to a study by John V. Moeser, professor emeritus of urban studies and planning at Virginia Commonwealth University.

Henrico County had 8.2 percent of its residents living in poverty, followed by Chesterfield County's 7 percent and Hanover County's 5.4 percent.

"These are urban issues," said Clara James Scott, principal of the Adult Career Development Center, which serves high school students who want a diploma, people seeking a GED [general equivalency diploma] and adults wanting career education.

Many of its students come from one-parent homes or live with siblings or on their own. Some are parents or pregnant. Most don't have role models, let alone work mentors.

"We don't have the creme de la creme," Scott said. "This may be the first person employed in their family."

In a career employment class, for instance, 21 of the 38 students are looking for jobs.

Transportation Problems

Another issue facing teens seeking work is transportation.

Brown can get to his job at Kings Dominion thanks to his mom, who usually gives him a ride. He often can grab a ride home with friends.

Not all teens are so fortunate.

"Transportation is a big thing," said Scott, the school principal.

Kings Dominion, for instance, is 24 miles from downtown Richmond and stopped offering employee buses between the park and the city several years ago.

Working close to home is key for low-income teens who rarely have transportation, said Valerie James-Gilbert, who teaches an education for employment class at the Adult Career Development Center.

Bus routes rarely run early or late enough or even to the right places, she said.

Communities Pull Together

Neighborhood groups have been trying to fill the gap in getting young people employable.

Price, the John Marshall junior looking for a job, lives with his mother and sister. His only job had been as a personal assistant to an elderly neighbor.

He needed experience and was referred to the William Byrd Community House, which runs a career program for 14- to 24-year-olds called Visioning for Success.

The course covers some basics: how to dress, how to behave at work, how to communicate.

But it also teaches about the economy and gets students to think about where they want their lives to go. After graduating from the program, they are placed in a summer job.

Price, 18, completed the program recently and will start his job—he hasn't been assigned yet—after the school year ends, as all participants do.

He considers himself lucky.

"I came here and they brought light into my eyes," said Jermaine Carrington, 19, who is going through the program now. "If you ain't got a plan, you plan to fail. You've got to do something."

Getting a job now is important to future job development, said Sum, the Northeastern University professor.

Teenagers fill out job applications. In 2010 teen unemployment reached its highest level since World War II.

The earlier a person goes to work, the better the outlook for future employment, he said. And getting a first job can be tough because employers tend to want people with experience.

"You don't work now, you won't work next year because you don't have employability skills," Sum said.

That increases the chances that teens will be "unemployed, underemployed and poor when they are 25," he said.

EIGHT

The Increased Minimum Wage Is Responsible for Record Teen Unemployment

Conor Sanchez

> Through a series of three increases from 2007 to 2009, the federal minimum wage in the United States has risen from $5.15 to $7.25. Some cities boast an even higher minimum wage. In Santa Fe, New Mexico, for example, the minimum wage was $9.50 at the time that this article by Conor Sanchez was originally published in the *Santa Fe New Mexican*. According to Sanchez, based on interviews with teens, business owners, and managers, the higher minimum wage has significantly reduced employment opportunities for teens. Reportedly, some employers now will not even accept applications from teens under eighteen. Others, particularly small business owners, say that with the higher wage, they want to hire more experienced workers and are less willing to hire teens new to the workforce.

School is out, and that means two things for teenagers—waking up late and finding a summer job. But for teens seeking to earn a little extra spending money, getting hired this summer [2008] may prove more difficult than years past.

Conor Sanchez, "Summer Bummer," *Sante Fe New Mexican*, June 3, 2008, p. D-1. Reprinted by permission.

Noah Kessler, a rising senior at Santa Fe [New Mexico] High School, is officially on the prowl for employment, but so far, it has been a fruitless endeavor. A few weeks ago, he walked into Beyond Waves Mountain Surf Shop on Cerrillos Road to ask if the shop was hiring for the summer, but the manager told him that unless he is over 18, he would not accept an application. The reason:

Santa Fe's $9.50 minimum wage.

Small business owners say that the higher minimum wage prevents them from hiring inexperienced teenagers.

Kessler, 17, has submitted applications to various hotels and restaurants across town in hopes of receiving a callback, but to no avail. "They called my girlfriend back because she's 18," Kessler said. "The only difference in our applications is our age."

If he does not receive a callback soon, Kessler says he may try to house-sit or mow lawns. If that fails, he says he wouldn't mind just kicking back and relaxing for the summer.

Fewer Teens Are Being Hired

Across Santa Fe, businesses are increasingly reluctant to hire teenagers, a trend that many attribute to the minimum-wage law. Small businesses, especially locally owned restaurants, have not only cut back on their payroll but on the amount of youth they hire as well. The deterioration of summer employment opportunities does not include competitive and often unpaid internships, but rather jobs typically occupied by inexperienced teenagers, such as busing tables, being a valet and scooping ice-cream.

Employers Want Experience and Maturity

Louis Moskow, owner of the Santa Fe Railyard Restaurant and Saloon and 315, said he has been turning away more applications this summer from teenagers compared to years past.

"This summer I am trying a different approach," Moskow said. "The way I see it, is when I employ unskilled labor for minimum wage, I'm not getting the most that I can in return. I'd rather pay double the wage for someone who's going to produce double the service because $9 an hour for someone who doesn't know anything means less to me than someone who can produce three times the amount. That is the result of the living wage. Because of that, I'm only choosing to hire skilled labor."

Moskow added that on top of being unskilled, teenagers lack the maturity deserving of a minimum-wage salary. Since he opened the restaurant in 2004, Moskow has terminated two teenage employees because they were talking on their cell phones too much. Ironically, it is jobs like these that are supposed to provide teens with their first lessons in working life, such as building confidence, exhibiting professionalism and gaining hands-on experience.

It is well documented that the majority of all minimum-wage jobs in the United States are held by people between the ages of 16 and 24. This age group also happens to be among the least educated and least experienced in the nation's labor force. It is no surprise then that an increase in the minimum wage has its greatest impact on the market for teenage labor.

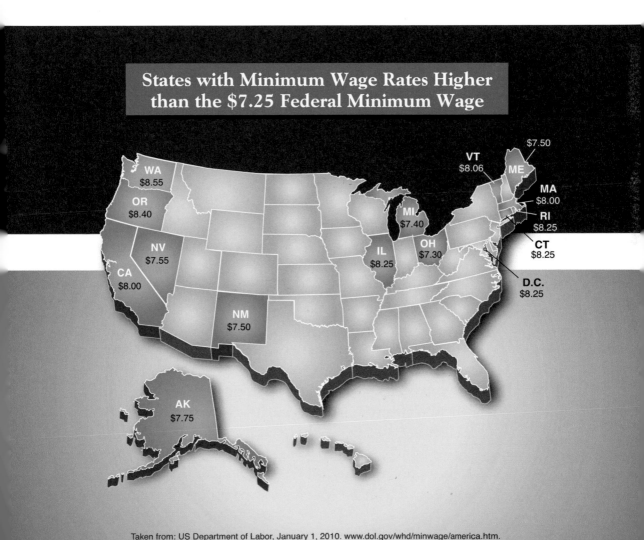

States with Minimum Wage Rates Higher than the $7.25 Federal Minimum Wage

$7.50

VT $8.06

ME

MA $8.00

RI $8.25

CT $8.25

D.C. $8.25

WA $8.55

OR $8.40

NV $7.55

CA $8.00

MI $7.40

IL $8.25

OH $7.30

NM $7.50

AK $7.75

Taken from: US Department of Labor, January 1, 2010. www.dol.gov/whd/minwage/america.htm.

The Rise in Teen Unemployment

According to the U.S. Department of Labor, Santa Fe's unemployment rate as of March 2008 was around 3 percent, a slight increase from preceding months. However, the unemployment rate among teenagers nationwide has risen from 15 percent in early 2007 to 18 percent. Many experts believe this is a result not only of the state of the economy, but also the recent increases in the U.S. minimum wage.

Simon Brackley, president of the Santa Fe Chamber of Commerce, calls this one of the unintended consequences of the minimum wage. While advocates view the policy as one way to raise the income of the working poor, businesses will be forced to consider the costs of hiring a new worker.

"It's not just the wage," Brackley said. "You have to consider worker compensation, Social Security and other expenses. When the economy is tight, as it is, businesses have to look carefully to see if they have the means to bring on a completely inexperienced new employee."

A Change in Wage Laws

Cindy Rogers, a career adviser at Capital High School, agrees that businesses throughout Santa Fe are not hiring as many teens. As a career adviser, her job is to match students with employment that corresponds with their interests, skills and abilities. However, as the wage laws have changed, so has the job market. Businesses that could previously be relied upon to hire teens no longer accept their applications.

"It used to be that businesses at (Santa Fe Place [Mall]) would hire teens but now that the living wage is in, they don't," Rogers said. "Larger department stores like Mervyn's still do, but smaller stores don't want to pay minimum wage to a teenager with no experience."

It is possible, as Rogers suggests, that the negative effects of minimum wage are limited to small businesses, and that larger businesses such as Mervyn's are not as harmed by the minimum-wage law. Shield Dux, who trains employees for Whole Foods Market on Cerrillos Road, says there has not been a decrease in the amount of youth hired for this summer season.

"I can't say that the Santa Fe minimum-living wage has had any sort of negative impact. Quite the reverse," Dux said. "One of our core values is team-member happiness. The living wage only supports that focus for our team members." Nevertheless, Whole Foods maintains a minimum hiring age requirement of 18 years of age.

Teen Unemployment Hurts Everyone

If the number of teens being hired for the summer season continues to decline, some fear it could have a number of consequences beyond high school and college. Brackley believes the minimum wage will have negative characteristics that impact the community as a whole.

"If teenagers can't find summer employment, they are more apt to getting in trouble," Brackley said. "We already have serious crime issues and if kids don't have a job to go to everyday, they're more likely to fall into temptation and get into trouble."

NINE

The Employment of Illegal Immigrants Is Responsible for Record Minority Teen Unemployment

Frank L. Morris Sr.

> With 16 percent of all black workers and 44.9 percent of black teen workers unemployed, Frank L. Morris Sr., a member of the board of directors of the Federation for American Immigration Reform, calls on the Congressional Black Caucus (CBC) and President Barack Obama to make changes, especially to reform immigration policies and enforce current immigration laws. According to this viewpoint, which appeared in the *Washington Times*, Morris believes that the most significant cause of the high black unemployment rates among young people is the lack of enforcement of illegal immigration policies under the CBC and the Obama administration.

Members of the Congressional Black Caucus (CBC) recently made the trip down Pennsylvania Avenue for a chat with a former member of the caucus, President Obama. According to news reports, it was not an entirely happy reunion.

Frank L. Morris Sr., "A Crushing Burden on Blacks," *Washington Times*, p. B-1, March 22, 2010. Reprinted by permission.

Like just about everyone else, it seems, the CBC has its own list of grievances with the man in the White House. Chief among the concerns of black lawmakers is the president's failure to address a black unemployment rate that far exceeds that of the general population. Sixteen percent of black workers are unemployed, and among black teens, a staggering 44.9 percent are out of work.

There is ample blame to be laid at the White House door, but the 43 members of the CBC who represent largely black constituencies also bear a large share of the responsibility. While some 8 million existing U.S. jobs are estimated to be held by illegal

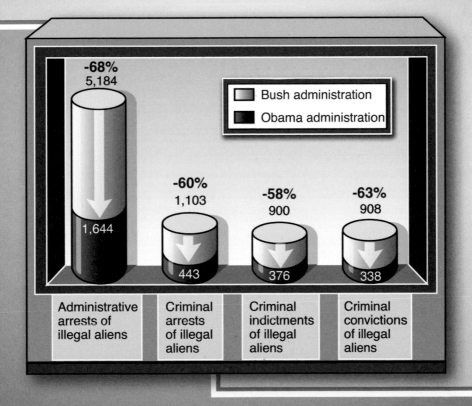

Enforcement of Immigration Laws Under Obama Administration Versus George W. Bush Administration

| | Bush administration | Obama administration |

-68%
5,184
1,644

-60%
1,103
443

-58%
900
376

-63%
908
338

| Administrative arrests of illegal aliens | Criminal arrests of illegal aliens | Criminal indictments of illegal aliens | Criminal convictions of illegal aliens |

Taken from: Frank L. Morris Sr., "A Crushing Burden on Blacks," *Washington Times*, March 22, 2010.

aliens, the CBC, like Mr. Obama, has consistently opposed tough enforcement of laws against employing illegal aliens. Many of the jobs filled by illegal aliens could be filled by black Americans, especially the huge cohort of black youth who are neither in school nor part of the labor force.

Rather than press the president to fulfill his responsibilities to American workers and resume meaningful enforcement against companies that employ illegal aliens, removing those workers from the country, the CBC marches in lockstep with the interests that promote illegal immigration. Since taking office last year, Mr. Obama has all but halted immigration enforcement in the workplace—a policy that enjoys the support of the CBC.

The CBC also has been front and center in the effort to enact amnesty for millions of illegal aliens and throw open the doors to still higher levels of future immigration. Late last year, representing her 42 colleagues, Rep. Yvette D. Clark, New York Democrat, whip of the CBC, stood shoulder to shoulder with Rep. Luis V. Gutierrez, Illinois Democrat, as he unveiled an illegal alien amnesty bill that would provide nothing for black Americans except more competition for jobs, educational opportunities and increasingly scarce government resources.

As members of the body that is crafting a federal budget projected to include $1.5 trillion worth of red ink, the CBC knows full well that we do not have the ability to spend our way out of the unemployment crisis that disproportionately affects black Americans. What they and the Obama administration can do, however, is make sure that American workers—regardless of race or ethnicity—have access to millions of existing jobs now filled by illegal workers, or any new jobs that may be created.

The CBC also should be the vanguard of the effort to reduce overall levels of immigration to the United States. During the 2000s, the growth of our labor force—fueled by the highest levels of legal and illegal immigration in our nation's history—outpaced the growth of jobs in our economy. As often has been the case throughout history, it is black workers who have suffered the most.

As leaders of the black community, members of the CBC are in a unique position to frame the immigration issue in terms of social justice and ensuring opportunity to all Americans. Latinos and other immigrants are not entirely to blame for unemployment that disproportionately afflicts black Americans. Rather, it is immigration policies that ignore the profound impact of millions of people entering our country—legally and illegally—that are a huge part of the problem.

Rather than compounding the damage that ill-conceived and unenforced immigration policies have inflicted on Americans generally and black Americans particularly, it is time for the CBC

Members of the Congressional Black Caucus (CBC) talk to the press at the White House after meeting with President Obama. The CBC criticized the president for not addressing the black unemployment rate, which far exceeds the rate of the general population.

and America's first black president to confront and reform those policies. Reducing immigration to the United States and enforcing laws intended to protect the interests of American workers are not only the right things to do, they are the only viable things to do given the fiscal realities our nation is facing.

Reforming America's dysfunctional immigration policies and enforcing laws against illegal immigration will not magically cure unemployment and other problems in the black community. But, under current circumstances, there is likely nothing that the CBC and Mr. Obama could do that would have more immediate or beneficial impact on black Americans. Sadly, it is a step that black congressional leaders and the White House are unlikely to take.

TEN

Cities Are Using Federal Stimulus Funds to Create Employment Opportunities for Teens

Carlos Becerra and Katie Meade

> With teen employment rates dropping drastically—from 46 percent in 2000 to 29 percent in June of 2009—large cities are using federal stimulus funds in an effort to help older youth find employment, according to Carlos Becerra and Katie Meade in an article for *Nation's Cities Weekly*, a publication of the National League of Cities (NLC). Becerra has assisted mayors in acquiring federal resources to support youth employment strategies, and Meade is an outreach associate for the Institute for Youth, Education, and Families, part of the NLC. Their article highlights measures taken in several large cities, where federal stimulus funds are being used to create programs aimed at lowering teen unemployment levels.

Embedded within the nation's weak employment numbers is a hidden crisis that has profound implications for the future economic strength of local communities.

The employment rate for teens has steadily declined since 2000, and in the current recession, teens face the lowest employment

Carlos Becerra and Katie Meade, "Youth Unemployment Rates Hit New Lows: Cities Tap Recovery Funds in Response," *Nation's Cities Weekly* 32 (32), August 24, 2009, pp. 1, 8. Reprinted by permission.

rate ever recorded in post–World War II history. In June of this year [2009], the teen employment rate was only 29 percent, compared to nearly 46 percent in June of 2000.

The latest data from the Bureau of Labor Statistics indicate that in July—a month when teen employment rates (not seasonally adjusted) are typically highest—only about one-third of 16- [to] 19-year-olds were employed in any type of job. A wealth of data suggests that such unprecedented lows in teen labor force participation may have serious long-term impacts on the youth who will become our nation's future workforce.

Low Employment Rates, Lasting Consequences

Youth employment is highly path dependent, meaning that if a young person is employed this year, he or she is more likely to be employed next year and into the future. According to the Center for Labor Market Studies at Northeastern University, the loss of cumulative work experience among teens who are not employed has adverse effects on future employment status and earning potential.

Recent findings from Northeastern University based on data from the National Longitudinal Survey of Youth suggest that each year of full-time teen work experience (2,000 hours per year) boosted annual earnings by 16 percent when those individuals reached their mid-20s.

Young men have been more severely affected by this downturn in employment. Between January and April of 2009, the monthly average employment rate for male teens was 26 percent, compared to just over 30 percent for females. Only 15 of every 100 black male teens were employed during these months. Jobless and economically disadvantaged males are more likely to drop out of high school, less likely to attend college and more likely to become involved with the criminal justice system.

While teens have struggled with joblessness, young adults also face serious employment challenges. For 20–24 year-old males, the average January to April employment rate was only 64 percent. Despite the fact that college graduates have managed to

The unemployed fill out online resumes at a job fair in Phoenix, Arizona, in November 2010. Young men have been more severely affected than other age groups by the downturn in the employment market.

maintain relatively high employment rates compared with their counterparts who have not completed college, only 50 percent of bachelor's degree holders (ages 25 and under) were working in the college labor market at the beginning of 2009, meaning the remainder were either jobless or employed in jobs that did not require a college education.

Tapping ARRA Funding

The American Recovery and Reinvestment Act of 2009 (ARRA) has steered large amounts of new funding—$1.2 billion—to stimulate youth employment. Many cities are collaborating with local workforce investment boards, nonprofit partners and educational

Large US Metropolitan Areas with the Highest Unemployment Rates

Metro Area	May 2010 Jobless Rate	May 2009 Jobless Rate	Year-to-Year Change
Las Vegas/Paradise, NV	14.1%	11.3%	2.8
Riverside/San Bernardino/Ontario, CA	13.9%	12.7%	1.2
Detroit/Warren/Livonia, MI	13.7%	14.9%	-1.2
Providence/Fall River/Warwick, RI-MA	12.1%	11.0%	1.1
Sacramento/Arden/Arcade/Roseville, CA	12.0%	10.6%	1.4
Tampa/St. Petersburg/Clearwater, FL	11.7%	10.5%	1.2
Los Angeles/Long Beach/Santa Ana, CA	11.4%	10.6%	0.8
San Jose/Sunnyvale/Santa Clara, CA	11.2%	11.0%	0.2
Miami/Fort Lauderdale/Pompano Beach, FL	11.2%	9.9%	1.3
Orlando/Kissimmee/Sanford, FL	11.1%	10.0%	1.1

Taken from: "Unemployment Rates for Large Metropolitan Areas." US Department of Labor. www.bls.gov/web/metro/laulrgma.htm.

institutions to use this funding to promote long-term labor market attachment for older youth in their communities.

For instance, the City of Sacramento, Calif., in partnership with its school system and workforce partners, has launched LINKS (Leadership, Integrity, Navigating choices, Keeping promises, Sufficient preparation), a program that combines paid work experience with the development of leadership skills.

Rather than coordinating a traditional summer jobs program, these partners have dedicated funding from ARRA to support counselors who promote a positive youth development framework, discuss future career options and serve as mentors.

Although many cities are experienced in offering summer jobs programs, ARRA's emphasis on older youth has heightened the importance of year-round activities. The City of Richmond, Calif., has used summer employment as a gateway for providing year-round services for disconnected youth. Upon completion of their summer employment program, youth with a high school diploma or GED [general equivalency diploma] will qualify for placement into the RichmondBUILD pre-apprenticeship construction training program or the YouthBuild program if they have not yet graduated. Both of these programs provide basic construction skills training.

Connecting Youth to Green Jobs

Several cities are capitalizing on ARRA resources and their own green economy ambitions to steer at-risk youth toward a new field of jobs in emerging industries. In Baltimore [Maryland], Mayor Sheila Dixon's Green Jobs Youth Corps provides 400 at-risk youth with paid summer employment focused on conservation and also incorporates an academic component. In tandem with the city's larger sustainability initiatives, youth are being trained on calculating carbon footprints, measuring air and water quality and retrofitting buildings.

Richmond youth are trained to provide home energy audits throughout the community and carry out low-cost energy conservation measures. In Seattle's Grey to Green Initiative, youth ages 14 to 24 have found jobs helping to protect watersheds and keep local rivers clean.

National League of Cities Assisting Twelve City Workforce Collaborations

NLC's [National League of Cities'] Institute for Youth, Education, and Families recently launched a Reengaging Disconnected

Youth through Economic Recovery Efforts learning community to assist 12 cities as they collaborate with workforce partners, connect with federal policy makers and plan strategies for youth employment.

Promising practices and lessons learned from this initiative will be shared regularly with members of NLC's Municipal Network on Disconnected Youth. Connecting youth to 21st century jobs will also be the focus of a workshop at the upcoming National Summit on Your City's Families in Boston on October 11–13 [2009].

ELEVEN

More Federal Relief Programs Are Needed to Decrease Teen Unemployment

PR Newswire

In 2008 the federal government instituted the Troubled Assets Relief Program (TARP) to address the subprime mortgage crisis that had contributed to the recession that began around 2008. In March 2010, with overall teen employment at an all-time low and with 83 percent of black teens and 75 percent of Hispanic teens jobless, teens marched to the US Capitol demanding their own TARP (Teen Age Relief Program), the PR Newswire reports. The article describes the Youth Unemployment Rally, key findings from the Center for Labor Market Studies, the community benefits of employed teens, and the blocked legislation that would have funded a summer employment program, which is what prompted the rally.

Teens laden with a 10-foot raft, buckets and life preservers marched today [March 23, 2010] to the U.S. Capitol during a Youth Unemployment Rally demanding a Teen Age Relief Program (TARP) to demonstrate before national, state and local government officials that teens are "sinking" due to record-level lows in teen employment rates.

PR Newswire, "Youth Demand Teen Age Relief Program (TARP) Bailout; US Capitol March with Life Preservers & Raft Demonstrates Rising Jobless Rate," March 23, 2010. Reprinted by permission.

Senators Who Voted Against Summer Youth Employment on March 9, 2010, and the Trends in Youth Joblessness for Selected States, 2000–2009 (Annual Average)

In the red states below, one or both senators voted against the summer youth employment amendment to the senate jobs bill. The amendment was defeated on March 9, 2010, and would have committed $1.3 billion in funds for summer employment programs.

"Like the national banks who received bailouts when they were sinking through the Troubled Assets Relief Program (TARP), youth need a TARP—the Teen Age Relief Program," said Jack Wuest, executive director, the Alternative Schools Network, a Chicago-based network of schools working with teens that have re-enrolled in school.

Teens marched from Stanton Park to the nation's Capitol demonstrating the impact of youth joblessness and the need for more

State	2000	2009	Percentage point increase in teen joblessness	Number of teen jobs eliminated 2000–2009	Number of teens employed by stimulus $ in summer 2009	Number of teens to be fired in summer 2010 by March 9 Senate Vote
Arizona McCain, Kyl [R]	53%	76%	+23	-80,278	2,925	2,925
Florida Martinez	56%	74%	+18	-167,099	13,250	13,250
Georgia Chambliss, Isakson [R]	54%	78%	+24	-123,611	11,020	11,020
Indiana Lugar [R]	49%	74%	+25	-97,540	2,560	2,560
Mississippi Cochran, Wicker [R]	62%	81%	+19	-32,705	6,542	6,542
Nevada Ensign[R]	53%	75%	+22	-29,656	1,466	1,466
New Hampshire Gregg [R]	41%	62%	+21	-15,385	516	516
North Carolina Burr [R]	55%	73%	+18	-92,953	6,396	6,396
Tennessee Alexander, Corker [R]	53%	74%	+21	-66,820	11,674	11,674
Virginia Warner & Webb [D]	52%	72%	+20	-87,395	3,535	3,535

Taken from: "Youth Demand Teen Age Relief Program (TARP) Bailout; US Capitol March with Life Preservers & Raft Demonstrates Rising Jobless Rate." PR Newswire, March 23, 2010.

jobs for teens across the country to increase the economic stability and future workforce development of the nation.

In late 2009, the national teen employment rate hit record-level lows, falling to 29.2%—a drop of nearly 16 percentage points from 2000 to 2009, according to a recent report, "The Lost Decade for Teen and Young Adult Employment in Illinois: The Current Depression in the Labor Market for 16–24 Year Olds in the Nation and State," conducted by the Center for Labor Market Studies at Northeastern University in Boston.

"No other age group has experienced such steep employment declines in the current recession. Youth depend on part-time jobs as a significant stepping stone to future employment, and they have been forced out of the job market and economically marginalized," said Deborah Shore, executive director, Sasha Bruce Youthwork. "We are running out of time to address the serious policy implications accompanying our jobless youth."

Last year, Congress voted $1.2 billion in the economic stimulus to employ jobless youth. More than 330,000 teens were employed, who without the stimulus funding would have been jobless and on the streets.

"We need to secure a broader stimulus plan and bailout for the teen job market," said Lori Kaplan, executive director, Latin American Youth Center. "Senators and political leaders need to understand the long-term and substantial impact of continued record youth joblessness. Job creation, particularly for teens and young adults, has to be a priority for 2010."

Making the Case for a Teen Age Relief Program (TARP) Bailout for Employment

From 2000 to 2009, employment rates among teens declined significantly in each gender, race-ethnic, family income, educational attainment, and geographic group, with male teens, Black teens and teens from low-income families hit the hardest with teen joblessness across the country.

Key findings from the Center for Labor Market Studies, Northeastern University included:

- Teen employment is at the lowest level in history.
- Teens are in a jobless depression.

- 83% of Black teens are jobless.
- 75% of Latino teens are jobless.

"Restoration of job growth for youth in the state and nation is critical and urgent. The statistics we've provided make a clear case for supporting national legislation to provide funds to create summer and year-round employment opportunities for 16–24 year olds across the nation," said Wuest. "Time is running out and immediate action is needed to provide a bailout in the form of $2.6 billion for jobs for jobless teens."

Youth employment is a key predictor of future success for the individual and the community, and directly correlates with youth violence and school dropout rates:

- *Stimulating the economy*—Every dollar earned is put back into the economy while helping individuals and their families.
- *Preventing violence*—Employed youth are engaged in their lives which often prevent them from turning to destructive interactions and illicit activities.
- *Building a future workforce*—Without employment, teens may never obtain the skills and experience they need, crippling their future and overall potential earnings.
- *Saving taxpayer dollars*—Keeping youth in school saves taxpayers $290,000 over the lifetime of each youth who graduates and earns a diploma.

Blocked Legislation

On March 9, 2010, U.S. Senator Judd Gregg (R-NH) demanded a procedural vote that led to the defeat of the amendment on the Senate Jobs Bill of the $1.3 Billion for Summer Youth Employment and $1.3 Billion for TANF [Temporary Assistance for Needy Families] Emergency Funds for Subsidized Employment. Funding for summer youth employment was just five votes short of the 60 votes needed to secure a subsidized [government funded] summer employment program for teens and adults.

In March 2009 New Hampshire senator Judd Gregg, left, was one legislator who effectively blocked an amendment to the senate jobs bill that would have allocated $1.3 billion for summer youth employment. Forty-one Republicans and four Democrats voted against it.

Forty-one Republican senators and four Democrats voted against this issue which led to the defeat of $2.6 billion for jobs programs for youth and adults. . . .

The youth at the March and Rally will particularly urge Republican senators to support this TARP employment program for teenagers. President Ronald Reagan's father, Jack Reagan, and brother, Neil Reagan, were suffering from joblessness at the height of the Great Depression in 1933. It was a particularly hard

Christmas for the Reagans in 1932, with Jack Reagan having been laid off from his job as a traveling salesman. In 1933, both Jack and Neil Reagan were provided jobs from the WPA [Works Progress Administration]. This helped them get back on their feet and restore their dignity by providing them with paying jobs.

The teens at this demonstration hope that the Republican senators will remember this when they consider another vote on providing jobs for teens who are stuck in a jobless depression. This only seems fair that if President Reagan's family received such significant help with jobs, that teens should receive help with employment this summer and year round.

TWELVE

Unemployment Will Have Lasting Effects on Today's Teens

US Congress Joint Economic Committee Majority Staff

> The US Congress Joint Economic Committee was established by the Employment Act of 1946 to make a continuing study of matters relating to the US economy. It is made up of ten US senators and ten members of the US House of Representatives; currently twelve are Democrats (the majority staff), and eight are Republicans. The committee holds hearings, performs research, and advises members of Congress. This viewpoint is an excerpt from a document prepared by the majority staff in May 2010 presenting research and information about the current state of unemployment among young workers. The excerpt explains the possible long-lasting negative consequences of unemployment over the lifetime of teen workers, such as lower wages and a decrease in productivity. The committee suggests that the government invest in the teenage workforce—by supporting actions such as job training programs—to lower teen unemployment.

Although the economy has gained strength and overall labor market conditions have improved in recent months [in the spring of 2010], younger workers have continued to struggle finding work. Employers added over half a million jobs in the last four

US Congress Joint Economic Committee Majority Staff, "Understanding the Economy: Unemployment Among Young Workers," May 2010. Reprinted by permission.

months, yet the unemployment rate for young workers reached a record 19.6 percent in April 2010, the highest level for this age group since the Bureau of Labor Statistics began tracking unemployment in 1947. . . .

The high rates of unemployment among young workers are cause for concern, and the effects can last long after the recession has ended. The "scarring effects" of prolonged unemployment can be devastating over a worker's career. Productivity, earnings and well-being can all suffer. In addition, unemployment can lead to a deterioration of skills and make securing future employment more difficult.

Research shows that young workers entering the labor market during a recession earn less than those who join the labor force during times of economic expansion. [Economics] Professor Till von Wachter recently testified before the Joint Economic Committee [JEC] that it may be 10 to 15 years before such a college graduate's earnings catch up to other graduates. For these graduates, the lack of employment opportunities makes paying off student loans a struggle. Graduates in 2008 finished college with an average of roughly $23,000 in student loan debt.

With the economy in recession in 2008 and 2009, student loans increased dramatically. Default rates on student loans also spiked. Demand for student loans has reached record levels, as the recession has forced more college students to take out loans and encouraged more students to stay in school rather than competing for a job in the weak labor market. Outstanding student loans have increased approximately 50 percent since 2007, according to data from the credit bureau Equifax Inc. Student loan defaults have also increased; in 2008, the default rate reached 7.2 percent, the highest level since 1999, and up from 6.7 percent in 2007 and 5.2 percent in 2006, according to the Department of Education.

Action Now Can Mitigate the Harmful Effects of Unemployment

The high unemployment rates faced by teens and younger workers during the recession may call for targeted policies to

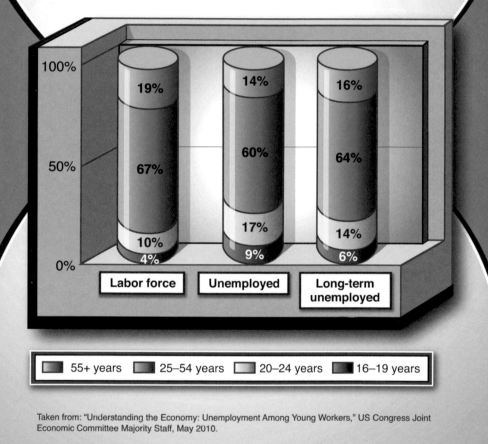

Young Workers Make Up a Disproportionate Share of the Unemployed and Long-Term Unemployed

These April 2010 percentages, which are not adjusted to reflect the differences between seasonal employment and school-year employment, show that young workers make up a greater proportion of the unemployed than they do of the labor force.

Labor force: 100% — 19%, 67%, 10%, 4%

Unemployed: 14%, 60%, 17%, 9%

Long-term unemployed: 16%, 64%, 14%, 6%

Legend: 55+ years | 25–54 years | 20–24 years | 16–19 years

Taken from: "Understanding the Economy: Unemployment Among Young Workers," US Congress Joint Economic Committee Majority Staff, May 2010.

help these workers find employment and regain their footing in the labor market. Acting now to implement policies that address youth unemployment will minimize the scarring effects for young workers, while benefitting society and the economy as a whole.

In the past four months, the economy has added 573,000 jobs, about the level needed to keep pace with population growth. While this marks significant progress from a year ago, stronger growth will be needed to significantly increase employment among teens and younger workers and to ultimately bring down their unemployment rates.

New graduates will benefit from training programs to ease the transition from school to employment and provide them with skills necessary to succeed in expanding sectors. For youth who have left the education system, programs are needed to keep them attached to the labor force while helping them acquire the skills needed to become, and remain, gainfully employed. Expanding financial aid programs can help young workers ease the financial burden of furthering their education, making higher education more accessible to all young people.

The significant investment in student aid made this spring is particularly timely. The Health Care and Education Affordability Reconciliation Act of 2010, which President [Barack] Obama signed into law on March 30, 2010, includes the largest investment in student aid in our nation's history. It increases the maximum annual Pell Grant to $5,550 in 2010 and, beginning in 2013, indexes the Pell scholarship to the Consumer Price Index, so that it keeps pace with inflation; channels all new federal lending to the Direct Loan program, saving taxpayers money; invests more than $2.5 billion in historically black colleges and universities; and invests $2 billion in community colleges through a competitive grant program that will help strengthen career training programs.

Beyond investing in financial aid for students, Congress passed the College Cost Reduction and Access Act in 2007 which allowed for income-based repayment of student loans for borrowers experiencing "partial financial hardship." Beginning July 1, 2009, loan repayment for eligible borrowers is capped at 15 percent of their discretionary income [money remaining after basic needs are met], which is reassessed each year. Any outstanding balance would be forgiven after 25 years. As part of the newly-signed

MAKING COLLEGE MORE AFFORDABLE

President George W. Bush signs the College Cost Reduction and Access Act of 2007. The bill made college more affordable for low-income students by increasing funding for Pell Grants by more than $11 billion.

health care legislation, Congress and the Obama administration lowered the threshold and maximum payments to 10 percent of a borrower's discretionary income, and shortened the period of repayment before any outstanding balance is forgiven to 20 years. Those changes will apply to new borrowers after July 1, 2014. Additionally, borrowers facing unemployment or other extreme economic hardship can also qualify for a deferment for up to three consecutive years.

Policies Can Mitigate the Harmful Effects of Unemployment

In addition, there are several policy actions that could help address the employment challenges facing younger workers.

- *Job Training*—As the labor market strengthens, expanded and improved job training programs may help young workers— workers who have had few prior work experiences—build and rebuild their skills. Better connecting job training to actual placement in a job is an area for potential innovation as is pairing unemployed individuals with corporations for training and employment. Paid internships that expose young people to new occupations and opportunities also offer promise.

- *Sectoral Employment Programs*—Relatively new to the workforce development landscape, these programs work with local employers to build skills necessary for employment in sectors of the local economy where there will be vacancies. Described by Dr. Lawrence Katz in an April 29 JEC hearing, these programs have gotten excellent returns by equipping unemployed workers with skills in demand in their communities. As more communities pursue this approach, particular attention should be paid to ensuring strong participation among younger workers.

- *Encouraging Mobility Among Young Workers*—To recover skills and wages lost during the recession, younger workers will need to be highly mobile across occupation and region. While younger workers are less likely to have mortgages and family obligations that can interfere with moves from one region to the next, they need to be aware of the importance of mobility to getting their careers back on track. Incentives that encourage young people to change occupations, when necessary, and to move to new, faster growing parts of the country could help young workers find jobs and boost their long-term earnings prospects.

- *Summer Jobs*—At the time of publication, Congress was considering the American Jobs and Closing Tax Loopholes Act which would add 300,000 summer jobs for young people. These jobs offer not just wages, but also provide valuable work experience to young people which can lay the groundwork for future employment.

Policymakers must be diligent in examining, understanding and offering innovative solutions to youth unemployment. In doing so, they can avoid a lost generation and instead create the next generation of productive American workers.

THIRTEEN

Teens Can Improve Their Chances of Finding Employment

CBS News

> With teen unemployment reaching 20 percent and beyond, prospects seem dim for young job seekers, especially as record numbers of unemployed adults compete for the same jobs. Finding a summer job is still possible, however, according to CBS MoneyWatch correspondent Farnoosh Torabi. In this viewpoint, a synopsis of her *Early Show* appearance in May 2010, Torabi explains that teens can increase their likelihood of finding employment by emphasizing the unique skills and flexibility of teen workers, investigating federal jobs, using their families to network, and contacting former employers.

The latest unemployment figures [as of May 2010] are encouraging: The economy added 290,000 jobs, the biggest leap in four years. However, unemployment for 16- to 24-year-olds stands at nearly 20 percent, and as the U.S. edges closer to the summer season, it may be more than 25 percent for teens.

Well you . . . can avoid this summer bummer, if you know where to look.

CBS MoneyWatch correspondent Farnoosh Torabi appeared on "The Early Show on Saturday Morning" with some great tips to help kids find jobs this summer.

CBS News, "How to Find a Summer Job," May 22, 2010. Reprinted by permission.

So why does the job picture differ for teens compared to the rest of the job market?

Torabi explained, "A new study confirms what we suspected all along was a major threat to young adults securing work in this recession: older workers."

Researchers at the Economic Policy Institute in Washington, D.C. found the size of the labor market fell more than six percent for young workers, while increasing more than eight percent for workers 55 years and older between December 2007 and January 2010. The teen unemployment rate in this country is more than 25 percent—more than double, almost triple the overall national rate.

She said, "Overall, the job market is not any better or worse for teens this summer, compared to last year. There's two problems: fewer job openings and baby boomers filling the jobs that would otherwise go to teens like part-time retail, working in fast-food, and assistant positions." And employers aren't necessarily hurting for cheap labor, according to Torabi.

She said, "The fact is, if you're 45 and suddenly out of work and need to pay your monthly mortgage, a job is a job is a job. Employers have the advantage now to potentially low-ball new hires—even if they have years of experience."

Torabi suggested teens try for jobs at large chains, such as McDonald's or Wal-Mart.

"These jobs are scarce but if you can get a job with a large retailer go for it," she said. "These places are known to offer great training and basic job skills. Plus, these types of retailers pride themselves in cultivating their employees and promoting from within."

Torabi also suggested these tips for young job seekers:

Play Up Your Teen-Specific Skills

Combat competition from the grown-ups by playing up your teen-specific skills. The top ways to compete against the older crowd is to 1) say you're totally flexible and 2) talk up your web and computer skills.

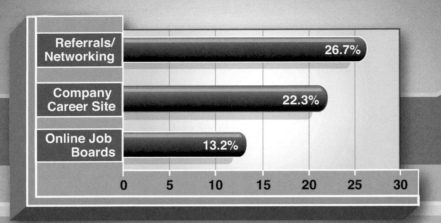

The Most Common Ways Companies Find New Employees

Referrals/Networking: 26.7%
Company Career Site: 22.3%
Online Job Boards: 13.2%

Taken from: Gerry Crispin and Mark Mehler, *CareerXroads 9th Annual Source of Hire Study: Meltdown in 2009 and What It Means for a 2010 Recovery*, February 2010, p. 12. www.careerxroads.com/news/SourcesOfHire10.pdf

This works great at delivery businesses (pizzerias) where you may have to work in the evenings and stores in the mall where they get a lot of traffic on the weekends.

Adults have more responsibilities and may not be able to work any and all hours of the week like you. And if you're a pro at social networking don't be shy about it. More companies are looking for young workers to help them market their brands online. Pizza Hut, for example, is looking for a TWINTERN this summer. Offer to do the same at some local businesses. Word on the street is that they're open to the idea.

Look into Federal Jobs

My federal sources say government jobs pay at least $10 an hour and the government has teen-specific openings. At jobsearch.studentjobs.gov you can look for federal jobs by city and state.

Jobs include: Helping out at the YMCA, lifeguarding, assisting at the local community centers, working in the mail room at the different military bases and more. This kind of work is getting more attention. Last summer the president's stimulus poured millions of dollars into the YMCAs, community centers, etc., just so these organizations could hire more teens. This summer they plan to hire again. Also if you go to a site like usajobs.com, you'll see dozens and dozens of listings for federal assistant jobs/clerical jobs for students at the various military bases in the country. For example, you can apply to work in the mail room at a local Navy base or be a life guard at a local Air Force base. Federal jobs pay an average $10 an hour—much better than minimum wage.

Ask Your Family to Get the Word Out

Ask your parents or older brothers and sisters to help you network through their LinkedIn profiles. On LinkedIn you can see all the

Researchers say that in today's economy teens have a better chance of finding jobs at large chains like Wal-Mart or fast-food restaurants.

people you know (and don't know) in your professional network. It's like six degrees of separation. With their help, hop onto their account, type in the company or business you want to work for and see who works there who may be connected to your family member in some way. And on Facebook, ask if your family can update their statuses to "My daughter or (younger sis) is looking for a part-time summer job. Would love your help!" (Incidentally this is what I did for my 19-year old brother and it worked!) . . .

Reapply for Your Job from Last Summer

More than 60 percent of part-time summer employers last year rehired their employees and the trend is expected to continue, so if you had a good time at your job last summer, chances are you might get your job back!

Ignore Rejection

REBOUND ALERT! Businesses like local banks, retail stores, amusement parks and vacation resorts, where jobs were scarce last summer, are showing a slight rise in hiring this year [2010], according to SnagaJob.com. So don't think that just because you got rejected last year you shouldn't try again. You may have better luck this summer. If you got rejected at Abercrombie and Fitch last summer, try again!

FOURTEEN

Teens Are Creating Their Own Employment Opportunities

Laura Petrecca

> Many teens are creating their own businesses—becoming their own employers, some because they have not been able to find part-time jobs and others because they would rather work for themselves, according to Laura Petrecca, marketing and advertising reporter for *USA Today*. Petrecca interviews the president of Junior Achievement USA to explain the trend and describes the success stories of several teen entrepreneurs, some who are currently teens and some iconic figures who started out as teen entrepreneurs. She also discusses skills that are necessary for success and some lessons teens have learned from their hands-on business experiences.

Eric Cieslewicz has spent the last couple of months drumming up business.

Faced with dismal employment prospects at traditional teen-friendly employers, the 18-year-old has turned his passion for percussion into a money-making venture.

The Milford, Ohio, high school senior set up a website promoting his services as a drum instructor, printed business cards and spread the word that he was open for business.

Laura Petrecca, "Don't Have a Job for Me? I'll Make My Own: More Teens, Stymied by a Tight Employment Market, Turn to Entrepreneurship," *USA Today*, May 19, 2009, p. 1B. Reprinted by permission.

He has eight students, ranging in age from 8 to 50. He hopes to pull in more than $400 a month from lessons, as well as earn more money from performing.

Amid shrinking job opportunities (the 16-to-19-year-old unemployment rate in April [2009] was 21.5%), many of his peers also are embracing their inner industrialist. The Small Business Administration's Office of Advocacy doesn't break out statistics for teens and tweens, but says in 2006, there were 492,000 people younger than 25 who were self-employed. Figures for that year are the latest available.

But experts say this year's number will likely rise due to job scarcity.

Already, the rough employment market has led kids to increasingly sign up for the entrepreneurial programs offered by youth-oriented groups such as Junior Achievement and the National Foundation for Teaching Entrepreneurship [NFTE].

"Kids are actively considering starting their own businesses," says Junior Achievement USA President Jack Kosakowski.

"It might be out of necessity, since there aren't a lot of jobs out there. But they're also seeing parents and other adults that have been loyal to companies for years . . . getting laid off, so these kids might be thinking, 'Hey, I might be better off being my own boss.'"

Success Stories

Many entrepreneurial kids will use their businesses to scrape together summer spending money, but the fledgling firms can blossom into something much bigger.

As a teenager, Tommy Hilfiger sold customized clothes in his Elmira, N.Y., hometown. Microsoft maven Bill Gates co-founded a data business that focused on traffic counts, Traf-O-Data, when he was in high school.

Today, consider Leanna Archer and Jasmine Lawrence.

As a grade-schooler, Archer, 13, often was asked about what product she used in her long, dark hair. She soon began to sell that all-natural hair-conditioning pomade, which comes from a

Home Depot chief executive officer Bruce Nelson addresses students about Home Depot's partnership with Junior Achievement to hire teens.

family recipe. She officially launched Leanna's Inc. from her family's home in Central Islip, N.Y., in 2005.

Business has gone so well, she's expanded her line of hair and body products to more than a dozen. . . . Imal Wagner, a public relations consultant who works for Archer pro bono [free of charge], says the firm pegs 2008 revenue at $110,000, and is on track to bring in more than $150,000 in 2009. A [business information provider] Dun & Bradstreet report puts annual sales at $140,000.

The impetus for Lawrence, who also founded a body-care company, was an unpleasant experience.

At age 11, her locks fell out after she used a chemical relaxer. Soon after, she was mixing up her own natural products.

At age 13, with savings from her allowance and a $2,000 loan from her parents, she started her small business, now called Eden BodyWorks.

Lawrence, now 17, says her company sells more than 20,000 units a month through a website alone. The products, which are produced at a facility in Harvey, Ill., have also been sold at retailers such as Wal-Mart.

She won't disclose sales numbers, but Dun & Bradstreet puts them at $740,000, and [business research company] Hoover's pegs revenue at $700,000.

Lawrence's mother, April, won't reveal revenue figures, either, but said overall sales have declined of late as the company contends with issues such as increased ingredient and transportation costs.

Organization Skills Prove Vital

The young businesswomen both cited a crucial tool that lets them run a successful firm yet still have teenage fun: an organized schedule.

Planning allows Archer to keep on top of homework and chores, yet have time to play sports and instruments such as piano and guitar. She checks orders on the computer after school, then makes adjustments to her schedule based on the daily demand for her product.

Lawrence, a high school senior in Williamstown, N.J., is involved in activities such as student council, tutoring and managing a basketball team.

"I'm still active like a normal teenager," Lawrence says. "But there are some times that I have to sacrifice time to do what I want for business needs."

Both also rely on a network of others to help them— including parents, siblings, teachers and paid help that includes family members as well as outside accountants. Non-profit group NFTE helped connect Lawrence with pro bono legal and financial advisers, whom she eventually hired.

That advisory squad is critical for success, says Bo Fishback, vice president of entrepreneurship at the Ewing Marion Kauffman Foundation, a group that focuses on entrepreneurship activities.

Archer says her family has given her fantastic feedback, as well as physical help as she concocts her beauty creams.

"He had a meteoric rise to the top."

"Meteoric Rise," cartoon by Joseph Farris. www.CartoonStock.com.

"When we make products in the basement as a family, it's kind of like a bonding time," Archer says.

On-the-Job Learning

Of course, selling can be tough work, Fishback says. But it teaches lessons. "If you get rejected 50 times as a 13-year-old, you get over it a lot faster than at 40. Trying and failing is one of the greatest learning lessons. . . . It breeds perseverance." That "experiential learning"—from successes and failures—will be valuable throughout life, he says.

Lawrence has had her ups and downs. A few years ago, she met a Wal-Mart contact at an entrepreneur-focused conference. That connection eventually led to her products being sold in 280 of the retailer's stores, she says. But that didn't work out for the long haul. Wal-Mart says it's no longer stocking Eden BodyWorks.

Drum instructor Cieslewicz says he's learning his share of lessons—such as how to keep an organized schedule and save receipts for tax write-offs—as he earns money for college.

"The hardest thing is lack of experience," he says. "It's all trial and error." Yet, he also says he's gleaning more than he would at a typical summer job.

"This is just the foundation for learning how to be a businessman," he says. "I couldn't learn this just working at a restaurant."

What You Should Know About Teens and Employment

Despite the fact that teen employment is at its lowest level in more than fifty years, millions of teens do still work. For those seeking jobs, the key consideration should be their own safety. With an average of fourteen workers dying every day in the United States and, in 2008, thirty-four teens under age eighteen dying in the workplace, it's important to know what the most dangerous jobs are and be aware of workplace dangers to which teens are vulnerable. Additionally, you also need to know your rights as an employee, including laws pertaining to sexual harassment, discrimination, and wages.

The Most Dangerous Teen Jobs

According to the National Consumers League, 2010's "Five Worst Teen Jobs" were:
- traveling youth sales crew
- construction and height work
- outside helper: landscaping, groundskeeping, and lawn service
- agriculture: harvesting crops
- driver/operator: forklifts, tractors, and ATVs

The Most Common Causes of Teen Workplace Deaths

According to the National Consumers League, of the ninety-seven teens under age nineteen who died on the job in 2008, the most common causes of death were:

- accidents involving motor vehicles
- accidents involving objects and equipment
- acts of violence
- exposure to hazardous substances or environments
- falling
- getting caught in or crushed by collapsing materials
- drowning

The Risk Factors for Workplace Injuries

According to the National Institute for Occupational Safety and Health, 70 percent to 80 percent of teens report having faced hazards in the workplace while working during high school. The institute also estimates that every year in the United States, 230,000 teens are injured at work, and of these injuries, 77,000 are serious enough to warrant trips to a hospital emergency room. According to the Occupational Safety and Health Administration, workplace injuries usually have one or more of these contributing factors:

- conditions that are stressful
- equipment that is unsafe
- safety training that is inadequate
- dangerous work that is illegal or inappropriate for teens
- supervision that is inadequate
- working too quickly
- working while under the influence of drugs or alcohol

Special Laws to Protect Teen Employees

To minimize the risks of teen employment, federal laws regulate the types of work that teens are allowed to do and the hours that teens are allowed to work during the school year and outside of the school year. Special laws exist to protect younger teens. Youth Rules!, a website for teen workers created by the US Department of Labor, provides the details of these laws. Below is a general outline of them with limited examples:

Prohibited Occupations

- Teens eighteen and older may work any job.

- Teens sixteen to seventeen may not work in jobs identified as hazardous by the secretary of labor, such as:
  - roofing or any other work on a roof
  - excavation operations
  - mining, except for coal mining
  - demolition or wrecking
  - manufacturing or storing explosives
  - forest firefighting, forestry, logging, or sawmill operations
  - operating power-driven machines, including woodworking; metal stamping, forming, or shearing; circular, band, or chain saws; hoisting; meat slicing or bakery machinery
  - driving or helping outside on a motor vehicle
  - anything involving radioactive exposure

- Teens fourteen and fifteen are prohibited from working in:
  - jobs identified as hazardous by the secretary of labor (see above)
  - manufacturing or mining, including coal mining
  - construction or repair
  - warehouse or storage work
  - peddling, door-to-door sales, or sign waving
  - any job requiring ladders or scaffolding
  - meat processing
  - cooking with an open flame; baking; or deep-fat frying, except with special equipment
  - transporting people or properties

These laws do include exceptions for some apprentice and student learners and for some agricultural workers, and individual states may impose additional restrictions.

Prohibited Hours
- Teens eighteen and older may work any days, hours, and number of hours whether the job is hazardous or not.
- Teens sixteen and seventeen may work any days, hours, and number of hours, unless the job is hazardous.

- Teens fourteen and fifteen may work only outside of school hours and only between the hours of 7 A.M. and 7 P.M., except between June 1 and Labor Day, when they may work until 9 P.M. Additionally, their hours are limited to:
  - three hours a day on school days, including Fridays
  - eight hours a day on nonschool days
  - eighteen hours per week during school weeks
  - forty hours per week during nonschool weeks

These laws include exceptions for students participating in approved work experience and career exploration programs and for some agricultural workers. Individual states may impose additional restrictions.

Rights Enforced by the Equal Employment Opportunity Commission

The laws enforced by the Equal Employment Opportunity Commission provide five basic rights for employees who work in the United States. If you work for an employer covered by these laws, you have the right to:

Work free of discrimination

Your employer, or potential employer, cannot make hiring, firing, promotions, training, wages, or benefits decisions based upon your race, skin color, national origin, religion, sex (including pregnancy), disability, genetic information, or age (forty or older).

Work free of harassment

This includes verbal, physical, or visual harassment, and it can take place at or outside of the workplace. The person doing the harassing can be anyone that you work with or for or someone else in your workplace, such as clients or customers. It is your right to be free of harassment based on your race, skin color, national origin, religion, sex (including pregnancy), disability, genetic information, or age (forty or older).

Complain about job discrimination without being punished

Request workplace changes for your disability or religion
You have the right to request changes that are reasonable and the right to expect your employer thoughtfully to consider making changes.

What You Should Do About Teens and Employment

In spite of the high rate of unemployment and other obstacles job-seeking teens face, there are things that you can do to increase your odds of finding a job. Furthermore, there are precautions you can take to stay safe once you find a job and steps you can follow if your safety and rights at work are being violated. There are even ways you can improve the state of teen employment in the world around you and make a difference for others.

You may be tempted to write off the job hunt before you even start, but do not be discouraged. Even though rates of unemployment, especially teen unemployment, keep setting new record highs, many teens *are* still working. Part of the low teen employment numbers may be due not just to lack of available jobs but also to unrelated trends: teens volunteering instead of working to bolster their college applications; teens being too busy because of the extra demands of advanced placement courses, dual enrollment, or college entrance exam courses; teens spending more time on extracurricular activities like sports and music; and teens experiencing increased responsibilities at home due to more single-parent and dual-income families.

At the same time, be realistic about your search. They call it job *hunting* for a reason. You cannot expect to apply to one or two places and instantly get hired—not even in a great economy. Apply to as many places as reasonably possible. Start with the places where you most want to work—those that are convenient, interesting, have a good reputation—and widen your net from there. If you have a friend with a job—a friend whom you think is appreciated by his or her employer—apply there and ask your friend to put in a good word for you. This networking is invaluable; it is said that one personal connection is worth applications to one hundred different companies. Do not stop with your friends, though. Tell your friends' parents and older siblings, your religious leader, and your next-door neighbor that you are looking for a part-time job. Use social networking sites to get the word out that you're looking for work. Other ways to get a foot in the door are with co-op programs through school and teen work programs through your community.

Keep your eyes open for places that employ teens, and apply to those places first. Also, apply to places that you visit frequently. If you primarily want to work during the summer, apply to places that are only open during the summer or that hire additional staff for the summer, like beaches, parks, orchards, and day camps. Also, apply to places where your youthfulness will be an advantage, and highlight that advantage on your cover letter, résumé, or application and when you interview. Examples of the benefits of young workers include a flexible schedule, technological savvy, abundant enthusiasm, physical endurance, patience with children, or the ability to memorize information quickly.

You should educate yourself as much as you can. Read your local newspapers and community newsletters and keep your eyes open for new or growing businesses in the area. Ask friends how they found their jobs. Read books, articles, and websites listed in the "Organizations to Contact" and "Bibliography" sections of this book for more job-hunting strategies as well as résumé, cover letter, and job-interviewing strategies.

One of the most important things that you should do about teen employment is to make sure that you are very familiar with safety issues and procedures. Before you start looking for a job, you should know which jobs are the most dangerous for teens so you can avoid them altogether. A list of the top five most dangerous jobs is published every year by the National Consumers League, and the 2010 list is printed in the "What You Should Know About Teens and Employment" section of this book.

You should also know current trends in workplace risk factors overall and which jobs are prohibited by the US federal government for certain age groups. This information often changes, so check the web pages of the National Institute for

Occupational Safety and Health, the Occupational Safety and Health Administration, and the US Department of Labor for updated information.

Whatever the job, there are key steps you can take to keep yourself safe. Never go to work overly sick or tired, or under the influence of alcohol, illegal drugs, or even legal drugs that impair your senses. Take your safety training seriously; take notes and ask questions. Follow your employer's safety guidelines, even the ones that seem silly and that no one else follows. Make sure that you know which hours and jobs you are allowed to work under federal and local laws for your age group. While your employer is responsible for not scheduling you to work longer than the mandated number of hours, or later than the specified hours (or later than the hours when you can safely work by yourself), as someone who is responsible enough to work, you must step up and remind your employer if he or she is violating this kind of legal boundary. Likewise, while your employer is responsible for not asking you to work a meat slicer if you are under age eighteen, you need to remind your employer respectfully of safety rules if you are under eighteen and are asked to do so.

If your employer does violate your rights or the rights of your coworkers, you should take action. If you have spoken with your employer and have not gotten anywhere, there are organizations that you should contact. Start with your union, if you are in one. If not, if you have a local Committee on Occupational Safety and Health group, contact it, or contact your closest Occupational Safety and Health Administration office. If wage, hour, or child labor laws are being violated, you should also contact your regional US Department of Labor's Wage and Hour Division office or your state's labor department. Two other organizations that work to protect minors are the Children's Safety Network Rural Injury Prevention Resource Center and the National Child Labor Committee.

Finally, use your voice to make a difference. Pay attention to workplace-related issues in the news by following your favorite news source or a website like the National Council for Occupational Safety and Health where you can track bills in Congress, learn about current campaigns, and find ways to become involved.

ORGANIZATIONS TO CONTACT

The editors have compiled the following list of organizations concerned with the issues debated in this book. The descriptions are derived from materials provided by the organizations. All have publications or information available for interested readers. The list was compiled on the date of publication of the present volume; the information provided here may change. Be aware that many organizations take several weeks or longer to respond to inquiries, so allow as much time as possible for the receipt of requested materials.

American Society of Safety Engineers (ASSE)
1800 E. Oakton St.
Des Plaines, IL 60018
(847) 699-2929 • fax (847) 296-3769
e-mail: customerservice@asse.org
website: www.asse.org

The ASSE works to educate teens about workplace safety almost daily through city events such as the annual Youth Rules! rally in Houston and other cities and by providing free resources such as a workplace safety guide for young workers, a work safety tips for teens handout, the ASSE teen safety tips web page, the safety suitcase for young children, and the annual ASSE safety-on-the-job poster contest for those aged five to fourteen. The ASSE also has student chapters and offers scholarships. Links to the abovementioned handouts, a Teen Work Safety Outreach PowerPoint presentation, and the interactive "Don't Be a Zombie at Work" online workplace safety game as well as additional educational resources are available through the ASSE website.

Cato Institute
1000 Massachusetts Ave. NW
Washington, DC 20001-5403

(202) 842-0200 • fax: (202) 842-3490
website: www.cato.org

Founded in 1977, the libertarian Cato Institute promotes the principles of individual liberty and free-market economics. Topics addressed by institute scholars include but are not limited to the economy, national security, and trade. In their analysis of the current unemployment situation, Cato scholars have denounced the government stimulus allocated to create jobs, charging that it has actually increased unemployment. Articles outlining this stance include "The 'Stimulus' for Unemployment," "A Second Stimulus Package? Yikes," and "Did the Stimulus Work?" Additional views from Cato on unemployment can be found in the institute's publications—the triannual *Cato Journal*, the quarterly *Cato's Letters*, and the bimonthly *Cato Policy Report*.

Heritage Foundation
214 Massachusetts Ave. NE
Washington, DC 20002-4999
(202) 546-4400 • fax: (202) 546-8328
e-mail: info@heritage.org
website: www.heritage.org

This conservative public policy organization promotes policies that espouse the ideals of free enterprise, limited government, individual freedom, traditional American values, and a strong national defense. Heritage scholars have conducted extensive research into the increasing unemployment rate, and their research can be found on the organization's website. Offerings include the "Heritage Unemployment Report: June Job Market Jolts Economy," "Unemployment Remains High Because Job Creation Has Yet to Recover," and "A Good Job Is Not So Hard to Find."

**National Institute for Occupational Safety
and Health (NIOSH)**
Centers for Disease Control and Prevention
1600 Clifton Rd.

Atlanta, GA 30333
(800) 232-4636 • fax: (513) 533-8347
e-mail: cdcinfo@cdc.gov
website: www.cdc.gov/niosh

The Occupational Safety and Health Act of 1970 created both NIOSH and the Occupational Safety and Health Administration (OSHA). NIOSH is part of the Centers for Disease Control and Prevention in the Department of Health and Human Services. The mission of NIOSH is to generate new knowledge in the field of occupational safety and health and to transfer that knowledge into practice for the betterment of workers. To accomplish this mission, NIOSH conducts scientific research, develops guidance and authoritative recommendations, disseminates information, and responds to requests for workplace health hazard evaluations.

National Youth Employment Coalition (NYEC)
1836 Jefferson Pl. NW
Washington, DC 20036
(202) 659-1064 • fax: (202) 659-0399
e-mail: nyec@nyec.org
website: www.nyec.org

The NYEC is a national membership network that improves the effectiveness of organizations that seek to help youth become productive citizens. Toward this end, the NYEC sets and promotes quality standards; tracks, crafts, and influences policy; provides and supports professional development; and builds the capacity of organizations and programs. Available on the NYEC website are links to a free online tool for program development, legislative updates, grant information, and research pertaining to organizations that help youth find employment.

US Bureau of Labor Statistics (BLS)
Postal Square Building, 2 Massachusetts Ave. NE
Washington, DC 20212-0001
(202) 691-5200
website: www.bls.gov

The BLS is the principal federal agency responsible for measuring labor market activity, working conditions, and price changes in the economy. Its mission is to collect, analyze, and disseminate essential economic information to support public and private decision making. As an independent statistical agency, the BLS serves its diverse user communities by providing products and services that are objective, timely, accurate, and relevant. Within the BLS website at www.bls.gov/audience/students.htm, many publications and resources appropriate for students are available, such as *Occupational Outlook Handbook*, *Occupational Outlook Quarterly*, "Career Information for Students," "U.S. Economy at a Glance," and the BLS Data Retrieval Tool.

US Department of Labor (DOL)
Frances Perkins Building
200 Constitution Ave. NW
Washington, DC 20210
(866) 487-2365
e-mail: cpsinfo@bls.gov
website: www.dol.gov

The DOL is charged with protecting the safety and rights of workers in the United States. Extensive information about wage and labor laws, unemployment insurance, health insurance and other rights of workers, and labor statistics is available on the DOL website. It also maintains a site, www.youthrules.dol.gov, with youth-related laws and information for parents, teens, and employers.

US Equal Employment Opportunity Commission (EEOC)
131 M St. NE
Washington, DC 20507
(800) 669-4000
e-mail: info@eeoc.gov
website: www.eeoc.gov

The EEOC is responsible for enforcing federal laws that make it illegal to discriminate against a job applicant or an employee because of the person's race, color, religion, sex (including pregnancy), national origin, age (forty or older), disability, or genetic information. It is also illegal to discriminate against a person because the person complained about discrimination, filed a charge of discrimination, or participated in an employment discrimination investigation or lawsuit. Most employers with at least fifteen employees are covered by EEOC laws. Most labor unions and employment agencies are also covered. The laws apply to all types of work situations, including hiring, firing, promotions, harassment, training, wages, and benefits. The EEOC has set up a special website for youth in the workforce, www.eeoc.gov/youth, with fact sheets, downloads, and quizzes that make equal employment laws easy to understand.

US Occupational Safety and Health Administration (OSHA)
200 Constitution Ave. NW
Washington, DC 20210
(800) 321-6742
website: www.osha.gov

With the Occupational Safety and Health Act of 1970, Congress created OSHA to ensure safe and healthful working conditions for working men and women by setting and enforcing standards and by providing training, outreach, education, and assistance. OSHA is part of the US Department of Labor. The Occupational Safety and Health Act covers employers and their employees either directly through federal OSHA or through an OSHA-approved state program. State programs must meet or exceed federal OSHA standards for workplace safety and health. Through its website, OSHA makes available publications including brochures and booklets, fact sheets, guidance documents, posters, QuickCards, standards, and more. Some publications are geared especially for teen workers. Individuals can also find regulations, submit a complaint, request that OSHA inspect their workplace, and ask questions through the OSHA website.

BIBLIOGRAPHY

Books

Peter Bielagus, *Quick Cash for Teens: Be Your Own Boss and Make Big Bucks*. New York: Sterling, 2009.

Jill Blatt, *The Teen Girl's Gotta-Have-It Guide to Money: Getting Smart About Making It, Saving It, and Spending It!* New York: Watson-Guptill, 2007.

Carol Christen and Richard N. Bolles, *What Color Is Your Parachute? For Teens: Discovering Yourself, Defining Your Future*. Berkeley, CA: Ten Speed, 2010.

Susan Griffiths, *Summer Jobs Worldwide, 2010: Make the Most of the Summer Break*. Oxford, UK: Vacation Work, 2010.

Anya Kamenetz, *DIY U: Edupunks, Edupreneurs, and the Coming Transformation of Higher Education*. White River Junction, VT: Chelsea Green, 2010.

Noreen E. Messina, *Teenwork: Four Teens Tell All: A Guide to Finding Jobs*. Tinley Park, IL: Goodheart-Wilcox, 2005.

Cynthia Shapiro, *What Does Somebody Have to Do to Get a Job Around Here! 44 Insider Secrets and Tips That Will Get You Hired*. New York: St. Martin's Griffin, 2008.

Kimberly Spinks-Burleson and Robyn Collins, *Prepare to Be a Teen Millionaire*. Deerfield Beach, FL: Health Communications, 2008.

Donald L. Wilkes, *Teen Guide Job Search: Ten Easy Steps to Your Future*. Lincoln, NE: iUniverse, 2006.

Periodicals and Internet Sources

Dina Berta, "EEOC: Industry Sued Most in Claims of Teen Harassment," *Nation's Restaurant News*, February 5, 2007.

Bureau of Labor Statistics, "College Enrollment and Work Activity of 2009 High School Graduates," April 27, 2010. www.bls.gov/news.release/pdf/hsgec.pdf.

———, "Employment and Unemployment Among Youth—Summer 2010," August 27, 2010. www.bls.gov/news.release/archives/youth_08272010.pdf.

Steven A. Camarota and Karen Jensenius, "A Drought of Summer Jobs: Immigration and the Long-Term Decline in Employment Among U.S.-Born Teenagers," *Center for Immigration Studies*, May 2010. www.cis.org/articles/2010/teen-study.pdf.

Brad Carlson, "Idaho's Teen Summer-Job Outlook Bleak: Older Workers Filling Positions Usually Held by Students," *Idaho Business Review*, May 18, 2009.

Current Events, a Weekly Reader Publication, "Help Not Wanted: Teens Suffer in a Tough Job Market," February 2010.

———, "Wage War: Should the Minimum Wage for Teens Be Lowered?" March 8, 2010.

Mediha Fejzagic DiMartino, "Economists Say Hike in Teen Unemployment Rate Related to Minimum Wage Increase," *San Bernardino County (CA) Sun*, March 5, 2010.

Deborah Donovan, "Ready to Work but Suburban Teens Find Tough Adult Competition," *Arlington Heights (IL) Daily Herald*, April 12, 2009.

Chris Farrell, "The Labor Market's Teenage Wasteland," *Bloomberg BusinessWeek*, August 10, 2010. www.businessweek.com/investor/content/aug2010/pi20100810_517982.htm.

Adrienne L. Fernandes and Thomas Gabe, "Disconnected Youth: A Look at 16- to 24-Year-Olds Who Are Not Working or in School," Congressional Research Service, April 22, 2009. http://ftp.fas.org/sgp/crs/misc/R40535.pdf.

Stephen Gandel, "The Teen Job Chop," *Time*, January 18, 2010.

Marjorie Hernandez, "Teen Unemployment Soars amid Economic Depression," *Ventura County (CA) Star*, December 4, 2009.

Human Rights Watch, "Fields of Peril: Child Labor in US Agriculture," May 5, 2010. www.hrw.org/en/reports/2010/05/05/fields-peril-0.

Katie Meade, "Mayors Make Summer Employment for Teens a Priority," *Nation's Cities Weekly*, June 9, 2008.

Teresa L. Morisi, "Youth Enrollment and Employment During the School Year," *Monthly Labor Review*, February 2008. www.bls.gov/opub/mlr/2008/02/art3full.pdf.

———, "The Early 2000s: A Period of Declining Teen Summer Employment Rates," *Monthly Labor Review*, May 2010. www.bls.gov/opub/mlr/2010/05/art2full.pdf.

Shannon Muchmore, "Blacks Rank Highest in Unemployment," *Tulsa (OK) World*, April 11, 2010.

National Committees for Occupational Safety and Health Network, "Health and Safety Rights on the Job for Teen Workers." www.masscosh.org/files/MassCOSH_TeenWorkerRights.pdf.

National Consumers League, "Teens, Avoid These Jobs in 2010," *Worker Rights*. http://nclnetorg/worker-rights/54-teen-jobs/401-teens-avoid-these-jobs-in-2010.

New Zealand Herald, "Teen's First Job Offers Vital Learning," March 20, 2010.

Catherine Rampell, "Teen Unemployment Rate Reaches Record High," *New York Times*, September 5, 2009.

Daniel Scherotter, "Mandated Wage Hikes Hurt Business Owners and Teen Job-Seekers," *Nation's Restaurant News*, October 5, 2009.

Vikki Sloviter, "How Dangerous Is Your Child's After-School Job?" *Pediatrics for Parents*, 2008.

Andy Smith, "Tough Times for Youths Seeking Summer Jobs," *Providence Journal*, May 11, 2008.

Patricia Smith, "$7.25 an Hour: Is It All Good News? This Summer's Minimum-Wage Hike Means More Money in the Pockets of Working Teens. But Is There a Downside?" *New York Times Upfront*, October 5, 2009.

Star-Ledger Wire Services, "Teen Employment Rate at Historic Low as More Parents Encourage Education, Activities," June

21, 2010. www.nj.com/business/index.ssf/2010/06/labor_figures_reveal_historic.html.

Andrew Sum, Ishwar Khatiwada, and Joseph McLaughlin, "The Consequences of Dropping Out of High School: Joblessness and Jailing for High School Dropouts and the High Cost for Taxpayers," Center for Labor Market Studies, October 2009. www.clms.neu.edu/publication/documents/The_Consequences_of_Dropping_Out_of_High_School.pdf.

Andrew Sum and Joseph McLaughlin, "Dire Straits for Many American Workers: The Economic Case for New Job Creation Strategies in 2010 for the Nation's Teens and Young Adults (20–24)," National Youth Employment Coalition, January 2010. www.nyec.org/content/documents/DireStraitsfortheNation's TeensandYoungAdults.pdf.

Mark Trumbull, "Why Teens Have a Hard Time Finding Summer Work," *Christian Science Monitor*, June 12, 2007.

Keith Wiedenkeller, "Future Shock: Meeting the Needs of Gen Y Employees," *Film Journal International*, June 2007.

INDEX

Gardner, Phil, 39
Gates, Bill, 91
Generation X, 35
Generations, 35
  are too diverse to
    generalize, 44–45
  imprecise definitions
    of, 42–43
  in workforce, 37t
Gen-Y. *See* Millennial
  generation
Gray, Mallory, 9–10
Green Jobs Youth Corps
  (Baltimore), 69
Green to Green Initiative
  (Seattle), 69
Gregg, Judd, 75, 76
Gutierrez, Luis V., 62

H
Handelman, Elise, 22, 24
Health Care and Education
  Affordability Reconciliation
  Act (2010), 81
Heavy-machinery jobs,
  25–26
Hilfiger, Tommy, 91
Honoring Emancipated
  Youth, 6
Howe, Neil, 34

I
Illegal immigration, is
  responsible for teen
  unemployment, 60–64

Immigration laws,
  enforcement under George
  W. Bush *vs.* Obama
  administrations, 61
Income, as factor in teen
  employment, 51
Injury Prevention Research
  Center (IRPC, University
  of North Carolina), 17,
  18
Institute for Youth,
  Education, and Families
  (National League of Cities),
  69–70
Iraheta, Juan, 5

J
Job training, 83
Jobs
  federal, 87–88
  heavy-machinery, 25–26
  outdoor, 24–25
  restaurant, 22
  retail, 22–24
  unconventional options,
    15
  See also Employment

K
Kaplan, Lois, 75
Katz, Greg, 13–14
Katz, Lawrence, 83
Kessler, Noah, 55–56
Kings Dominion, 50, 52
Kosakowski, Jack, 91
Kugell, Jaclyn, 28, 33

PICTURE CREDITS